Absolute Beginner's Guide to Access™

Absolute Beginner's Guide to Access™

Greg Perry

SAMS
PUBLISHING

A Division of Prentice Hall Computer Publishing
11711 North College, Carmel, Indiana 46032 USA

To Dr. Robert Gray: You always keep me well so that I can write. Thanks! It's nice to have a doctor who is also a friend.

Copyright © 1993 by Sams Publishing

International Standard Book Number: 0-672-30366-3

Library of Congress Catalog Card Number: 93-84390

96 95 94 93   4 3 2 1

Interpretation of the printing code: the rightmost double-digit number is the year of the book's printing; the rightmost single-digit, the number of the book's printing. For example, a printing code of 93-1 shows that the first printing of the book occurred in 1993.

Composed in Palatino, Dom Casual, Helvetica, and MCPdigital by Prentice Hall Computer Publishing

Printed in the United States of America

Trademarks

Overview

Introduction

Part I   Getting Ready for Access

1   What's Access All About? Access Is a Database
Management System

2   Where Do I Begin? Put Design in Your Data

3   How Do I Install Access? Access Installs Itself

4   How Can I Get Help? Check Out Help and Cue Cards

Part II   Getting Acquainted with Access

5   What Do I Do First? Create a Database and Learn the Tools

6   How Do I Create Tables? Use the Table Object's Button

7   How Do I Describe Fields? Use the Table Definition Window

8   What Are the Three Rules of Proper Computing?
Back Up, Back Up, and Back Up

9   Can I Change a Table Definition? Access Enables You to
Rearrange Your Tables Easily

Part III   Working with the Data

10   How Do I Put Data in a Table? Use the Datasheet View

11   Can I Manage Several Records? Enter and Look Through
the Datasheet View

12   What Is a Form? A Form Is Another View of Table Data

13   Can I Print Data? Use Access's Simple Printer Output

Part IV   Honing Your Skills

14   Can I Do More with a Datasheet? Use Advanced
Datasheet Commands

15   How Do I Improve My Form's Appearance?
By Customizing Your Forms

Part V   Querying the Database

16   What Is a Query? A Query Is Just a Database Question

17   What More Can I Do with Queries? Use Relational Operators

18   How Do Queries Work with Forms? Forms and Complex Queries Go Well Together!

Part VI   Multiple Tables

19   How Do I Add More Tables? Relate Them If You Can

20   How Can I See Two Tables? Use a Multiple-Table Query

21   Will a Form Work with Two Tables? Use a Subform: A Form Within a Form

Part VII   Advanced Reporting

22   How Do I Create Reports? ReportWizards Makes Report-Writing Easy

23   How Do I Print Mailing Labels? Design and Print the Label

Part VIII   Advanced Access

24   Can Access Draw Graphs? Access Creates Beautiful Graphs from Your Database

25   What Lies Ahead? Advanced Database Development, Macros, and Programming

A   Glossary

B   Where Do I Go from Here?

Index

Contents

Introduction xix

Part I Getting Ready for Access

1 What's Access All About?
Access Is a Database Management System 3

A Database Is Where It's At 5
How Is Access Different? 7
Still Confused? 9
Chapter Wrap-Up 10

2 Where Do I Begin? Put Design in Your Data 13

Getting a Grip on Databases 14
Breaking the Database into Tables 16
The Format of Tables 17
The Key to Understanding 19
What Now? 21
Chapter Wrap-Up 21

3 How Do I Install Access? Access Installs Itself 25

Installing Access 26
Starting and Stopping Access 29
Chapter Wrap-Up 32

4 How Can I Get Help? Check Out Help and Cue Cards 33

Help Is a Keystroke Away 34
Getting More Help 37
Searching for Help 38
Context-Sensitive Help 39
Cue Cards Extend Help 40
Magic Wizards 41
Chapter Wrap-Up 41

Part II Getting Acquainted with Access

5 What Do I Do First? Create a Database and Learn the Tools 45

Filing Your Database 46
This Book's Sample Database 47
Creating the Database File 48

The Database Window 50
The Table Object 51
The Query Object 52
The Form Object 53
The Report Object 54
The Macro and Module Objects 55
Looking Around 55
Chapter Wrap-Up 56

6   **How Do I Create Tables?** Use the Table Object's Button   59

Creating the Table Structure 61
A Word on Field Characteristics 62
A Hands-On Table Structure Definition 66
Chapter Wrap-Up 68

7   **How Do I Describe Fields?** Use the Table Definition Window   71

Describing the Fields 72
If You Make Mistakes 76
Specifying Other Data Types 77
Defining More Field Properties 78
Specifying the Primary Key 80
Finishing the Table Definition 81
Chapter Wrap-Up 82

8   **What Are the Three Rules of Proper Computing?**
Back Up, Back Up, and Back Up   85

Getting Ready to Back Up 86
Making a Windows Backup 88
You're Now Practicing Safe Computing! 91
Chapter Wrap-Up 92

9   **Can I Change a Table Definition?**
Access Enables You to Rearrange Your Tables Easily   93

Preparing to Change the Table's Structure 94
Adding Fields 95
Adding Fields Behind the Others 96
Inserting New Fields Between Existing Ones 97
Deleting Fields Is a Snap 98
Messing with the Table 100
Chapter Wrap-Up 103

Part III   Working with the Data

10   How Do I Put Data in a Table? Use the Datasheet View   107

Getting Ready to Enter Data 108
The Datasheet View 110
Let's Enter Some Data 111
Special Data Considerations 114
Managing the Datasheet 115
Chapter Wrap-Up 117

11   Can I Manage Several Records?
Enter and Look Through the Datasheet View   119

Getting More Data In 120
Moving Around 127
Getting a Bird's-Eye View 129
Deleting Records 130
Chapter Wrap-Up 131

12   What Is a Form? A Form Is Another View of Table Data   133

Get Ready to Be Amazed! 135
Moving Around with Forms 139
Changing Data 140
Adding Data 141
Deleting Records in Form View 142
Save Your Work! 142
Chapter Wrap-Up 143

13   Can I Print Data? Use Access's Simple Printer Output   145

Printing from the Datasheet 146
Modifying the Output 148
Printing from Forms 150
Chapter Wrap-Up 152

Part IV   Honing Your Skills

14   Can I Do More with a Datasheet?
Use Advanced Datasheet Commands   155

Finding a Needle in the Stack of Data 156
Replacing Data 159
Hiding Fields 161
Format Your Data 162
One Last Datasheet Change... 164
Chapter Wrap-Up 164

15   How Do I Improve My Form's Appearance?
     By Customizing Your Forms   167

     Always Start with FormWizard 168
     Working with the Form Design 169
          Changing the Form's Colors 170
          Changing the Form's Field Locations 172
          Changing the Form's Field Sizes 175
     Chapter Wrap-Up 177

Part V   Querying the Database

16   What Is a Query? A Query Is Just a Database Question   **181**

     Building a Query 182
          Preparing for the Query 183
          Selecting Fields 184
          Asking the Query 186
     Chapter Wrap-Up 188

17   What More Can I Do with Queries?
     Use Relational Operators   189

     Meeting Your Match 190
     Extending the Criteria 193
     Chapter Wrap-Up 195

18   How Do Queries Work with Forms?
     Forms and Complex Queries Go Well Together!   197

     Combining Relations: The Logical Operators 198
          The AND Operator 199
          Using BETWEEN 200
          The OR Operator 200
     One More Major Query Step 201
     Linking a Form to a Query 205
     Chapter Wrap-Up 207

Part VI   Multiple Tables

19   How Do I Add More Tables? Relate Them If You Can   **211**

     Friendly Relatives 212
          One-to-One Table Relationships 213
          One-to-Many Table Relationships 214
          Many-to-Many Table Relationships 216

Adding a Table 217
Putting Data in the Table 218
Chapter Wrap-Up 222

20 How Can I See Two Tables? Use a Multiple-Table Query   **225**

The Makeup of a Multiple-Table Query 227
Creating the Query 228
Fixing a Problem 231
Turning a Dynaset into a Table 233
Chapter Wrap-Up 235

21 Will a Form Work with Two Tables?
Use a Subform: A Form Within a Form   237

Relate the Tables First 238
Creating a Subform 240
Chapter Wrap-Up 244

Part VII   Advanced Reporting

22 How Do I Create Reports?
ReportWizards Makes Report-Writing Easy   249

Be a Wizard with ReportWizards 250
Adding Some Grouping 254
Chapter Wrap-Up 257

23 How Do I Print Mailing Labels? Design and Print the Label   **259**

What Do You Want? 260
Let's Play Post Office 261
Chapter Wrap-Up 268

Part VIII   Advanced Access

24 Can Access Draw Graphs?
Access Creates Beautiful Graphs from Your Database   271

Let's Draw 273
Getting a Little Bolder 275
Get to Work and Play! 277
Chapter Wrap-Up 278

25   **What Lies Ahead?** Advanced Database
         Development, Macros, and Programming   **279**

         Taking a Ride with Northwind Traders 281
         True Automation 282
         Macros: Your Next Step 285
         Chapter Wrap-Up 286

A   **Glossary**   **287**

B   **Where Do I Go from Here?**   **293**

Index   **295**

Acknowledgments

I have made it a practice in my past few books to praise the people at Sams Publishing, and this will be no exception. Dear readers, the people at Sams want you to have the best book possible, and all their efforts go into that goal. I cannot begin to explain how grateful I am to have worked with Stacy Hiquet over the past year and a half. She (like all the editors at Sams) is a friend who makes a tiresome writing day better with a cheerful voice. Scott Parker keeps my writing accurate when I waiver. Dean Miller lends direction when I miss it. Cheri Clark and Gayle Johnson edit with style and grace. Jordan Gold and Richard Swadley provide the high-level guidance that makes everything work well.

My writing is directly enhanced by my readers through the years. Although I cannot begin to answer most of the cards and calls I get, I keep writing books because of the good things that I keep hearing about them.

Jayne, my beautiful bride, and my parents, Glen and Bettye Perry, teach me every day that support is better than gold.

About the Author

Greg Perry is a speaker and writer in both the programming and the applications sides of computing. He is known for being able to bring programming topics down to the beginner's level. He received his first degree in computer science, followed by a master's degree in corporate finance. Besides writing, he teaches, consults, and lectures across the country, including the acclaimed Software Development conferences. Perry is the author of almost 20 other computer books, including *Absolute Beginner's Guide to Programming, Absolute Beginner's Guide to QBasic, Absolute Beginner's Guide to C, Moving from C to C++,* and *Turbo C++ Programming 101* (all published by Sams Publishing). In his spare time, he gives lectures on traveling to Italy, his second-favorite place to be.

Introduction

Do you have unwieldy data? Would you like to add some organization to your organization? Does your Information Systems department cry every time you request a report? Does this paragraph sound like an advertisement? It is! This is to advertise that you now have the power to take control of your data. Microsoft Access turns data spaghetti into an ordered informational system.

The Microsoft Corporation threw the microcomputer community a curveball when it introduced the Microsoft Access for Windows database. The world is still digesting the Access feast for database users and programmers. Most of the Access world is divided into two groups of people: advanced database users who need the power that Access provides, and introductory users who need to know *nothing* about the database programming but simply need to create, store, change, remove, and look at their data in an orderly and easy manner. This book rescues that second group of people. Guess what? This book helps prepare people to become advanced users as well!

Access does not have to be difficult. Even computer novices—no, even people who *hate* computers—can learn Access quickly and easily! It only takes a book to speak at your level, but not down to you. The book you now hold laughs as much at itself as it does at Access, and if you come along for the ride, you'll have fun, you'll learn the basics of Access, and you'll gain some fundamental insight into the professional world of database users as well.

Why Is This Book Different?

Absolute Beginner's Guide to Access breaks the commonality of computer books by talking directly to you. This book is like having your best friend sitting next to you teaching you Access. *Absolute Beginner's Guide to Access* attempts to *express* without having to *impress*. This book talks to you in plain language, not computerese.

This book, with its short chapters, line drawings, helpful screen shots, and straight talk, makes your trip through the maze of Access faster, friendlier, and easier than any other book available today.

Do You Know Enough?

This is a beginner's book. If you have never used a database program, this book is for you. No knowledge of any database concept is assumed. If you can't even manage your own checkbook, you can learn to use Access with this book.

The term *absolute beginner* has different meanings at different times. You might be new to computers. You might never have used a database before in your life. You might have used other databases but found them to be complex. If so, read on, o faithful one, because in 25 quick chapters, you'll know Access.

What Makes This Book Different?

This book does not cloud issues with internal technical stuff that Access newcomers don't need. This author is of the firm belief that introductory principles have to be taught well and slowly. After you tackle the basics, the "harder" parts never seem hard. This book teaches you the real Access that you need in order to get started and does not get into the specifics that a newcomer has no need for.

Any subject is easy if explained properly. Nobody can teach you anything, because you have to teach yourself, but if the instructor, book, or video doing the teaching doesn't make the subject simple and *fun,* you won't *want* to learn the subject. You won't believe how easy, straightforward, and fun Access can be until you see it for yourself in these pages.

Conventions Used in This Book

The following typographic conventions are used in this book:

- Commands you type and any text you see on-screen are in monospace.

- Filenames are in regular text, all uppercase (RENTAL.MDB).

- New terms appear in *italic*.

- Hot keys appear in color.

Index to the Icons

Like many computer books, this book contains lots of helpful hints, tips, and warnings. You will run across many *icons* (little pictures) that bring these specific items to your attention. A glance at the icon gives you a quick idea of the purpose of the text next to the icon.

Here are descriptions of this book's icons:

YIKES!

This icon points out potential problems you could face with the particular topic being discussed. Often, the icon indicates a warning that you should heed or provides a way to fix a problem that might occur.

PSST! All this book's hints and tips (and there are lots of them) are highlighted by this icon. When a really neat feature or Access trick coincides with the topic you are reading about, this icon pinpoints just what you can do to take advantage of the added bonus.

HMM... Throughout Access, some subjects offer a deeper level of understanding than others. This icon lets you know about something you might not have thought about, such as a new use for the topic being discussed.

Skip This, It's Technical

If you don't want anything more than the beginning essentials of Access, don't read the material next to this icon. Actually, most of you will enjoy this material, but be aware that you can safely skip it without losing the meaning of the chapter.

Can I See Access Work Right Away?

Unlike many books, this book puts you to work early looking at examples and designing an Access database in the first section of the book. You must learn Access hands-on; there is no other way. Some people have learned complete programming languages without a computer, but Access requires that you sit in front of your computer screen, digesting the items there.

Not only are database concepts and Access techniques taught in every chapter of this book, but you will see a sample application being created as you progress through the book. You will also see references to the sample Northwind Traders database that comes with Access so that you can see other (and often more advanced) ways of accomplishing something you need to do.

There are almost always several ways of completing the same task in Access. Although a mouse click is often faster, you can use the keyboard alone for most of your work.

What Access Application Does This Book Create?

A special database is created throughout this book for *Laura Landlady's Rental Properties,* a make-believe rental property empire. The owner, Laura, has been building her rental property business for the past few years and is buried in data. To organize her records, Laura has turned to Access. Before she knows it, Laura's Access application will have organized her records and streamlined her day-to-day bookkeeping.

You might not need to organize the same type of database as Laura, but that doesn't matter. Many books and classes out there create specific applications, and the students sit by, going through the motions of developing an application they'll never use. Laura's application is built from scratch in the *same way* that you would approach an application of your own. Even if Laura's specific database isn't like the one you need, there will be a one-to-one correspondence between Laura's quest for a database and yours because of the questions answered and the tasks accomplished.

What If I've Never Touched a Computer?

If you've never touched a computer, Access is not necessarily a bad place to begin—with one slight caveat: Access is a fully integrated Windows program. Windows is the operating environment that

Access works within. If you are new to computers or Windows, you might have some difficulty getting around in Access. You don't have to be an expert in Windows, or even fairly well versed, but you should have done some work in Windows (or read a good book or two on Windows) before starting this book.

If you've never touched a computer before, pick up a quick beginner's book on DOS or Windows. Good beginner's books such as *I Hate DOS* (Que, 1993) and *Fear Windows No More* (Brady, 1993) will acquaint you with disks, files, the keyboard, the mouse, and the Windows environment. Windows was created for beginners, and one of the goals of Windows is that if you learn one Windows program such as Access, you then will feel comfortable with almost every other Windows program interface.

If you are not new to computers but you are new to Windows, one of the best ways to learn about the mouse and Windows is to play the Solitaire game that comes with Windows. Solitaire will hone your mouse skills and show you that a Windows program can be fun.

What Do I Do Now?

Turn the page and learn Access.

Part I
Getting Ready for Access

What's Access All About?

Access Is a Database Management System

- A Database Is Where It's At 5
- How Is Access Different? 7
- Still Confused? 9

Computers do best what people like least. Computers can sift through countless reams of data, filtering, reporting, and analyzing whatever needs to be filtered, reported, and analyzed. People find that sifting through a bunch of data is boring. Once the computer has done this boring job, a person can make insightful decisions based on the computer's results. A computer can't think on its own and make intuitive decisions, despite what some people might lead you to believe. A computer is only a tool that you must instruct, direct, and review much more closely than any human personnel.

Data is a general term for facts and figures. *Information* is processed data. A computer program, if properly written, can analyze a bunch of unrelated facts and figures and report relationships, sort values, and produce meaningful information for people who must make decisions based on that information.

HMM... The term *data*, although plural for the singular *datum*, is used for both the singular and the plural in this book. This way, you won't have to read about your "datum value" and your "data values." Proper grammar moves aside here to keep the text flowing.

Microsoft Access's goal is to turn raw data into meaningful information. Too many people suffer from "information overload." In today's world, too much data gets in the way of the information we need. As Figure 1.1 shows, Access turns your data into meaningful information.

PSST! Don't drown in data. Let Access do the boring dirty work processing the details. Access can give you the information you need from the data that floods your working life. You then can analyze the results from Access's tedious work and be a hero or heroine to those you work with who can't get on top of overwhelming data.

Figure 1.1.

Access sorts through all the messy details (data) and gives you answers (information) that you need.

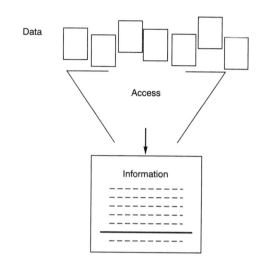

A Database Is Where It's At

A *database* is any collection of data. A database doesn't have to be computerized. A card file of recipes is a database. An inventory listing is a database. A filing cabinet is a database. A database is any collection of data values that relate to each other. A database provides some way for the user to get to data that is needed. For example, an inventory listing might be sorted in the order of part numbers. When you want to know the quantity of an item, you can scan through a listing printed by part numbers until you get to the inventory item you want to know about.

A computer is the perfect database holder. As mentioned earlier in this chapter, computers are great for sifting through many facts and figures. When an inventory database is computerized, you don't have to look through a list to find the quantity you need—you only have to ask the computer to do the finding for you.

A computerized database does more than search for values. A computerized database produces information in any combination and sorts it in any order. A computerized database enables you to add more data to the database, change data that's already there, and remove unwanted data.

Perhaps the best reason to computerize your database needs with Access is that the user of the database doesn't need to know anything about the data's structure or the computer behind the data. Of course, the creator of the database has a good idea of how the data is formatted, but someone using Access doesn't have to be an Access pro, as Figure 1.2 shows.

Figure 1.2.

The users of Access don't have to know anything about Access or the way the database is stored.

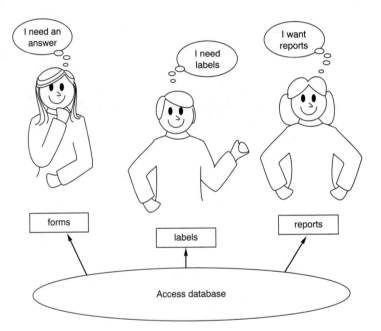

You'll see the term *user* throughout this text. The user of Access is you and anyone else who might have to get information from an Access database. Users sometimes are called *end users*.

How Is Access Different?

There are many computer database programs on the market, and they all provide tools that keep track of large amounts of data, filtering through the data and providing the answers people need. Access is one of the first to integrate fully with the Microsoft Windows environment (both Access and Windows were written by Microsoft). Access consists of a graphical environment. That is, instead of issuing commands, you often just point and click with the mouse pointer to get work done.

PSST!

Once you learn one Windows application, such as Access, you understand the interface of all Windows applications. With non-Windows, DOS-based programs, each program might interface with you in a different way. If you're familiar with a Windows program, however, you'll be able to make the transition to Access rapidly.

Access provides several *WYSIWYG* (pronounced WIZZ-ee-wig) tools like those you may have seen in word processors. WYSIWYG stands for *what you see is what you get*. As you design an Access data-entry form or report, you can request a preview of the form or report on the screen. For example, Figure 1.3 shows a preview of a report on the screen before it's printed. Although you can't read the fine print, you can check the report's overall appearance before sending it to the printer.

 **HMM...**

The fast feedback that WYSIWYG provides means that you'll design applications more quickly and be able to get home from work earlier!

Figure 1.3.
Previewing a report before printing it.

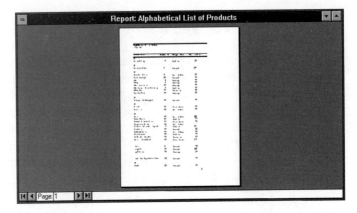

Perhaps the most important advantage Access provides is that it is a *relational database management system (RDBMS)*. RDBMS is a fancy term that means different things depending on how it's implemented. Access implements the primary RDBMS advantage by storing all database data in one place on disk. Although you might look at your data in many different formats, and although you have several ways of changing that data, when you make a change, that change is stored in one place so that all other views of the data will reflect the same answers.

YIKES!

RDBMS? Computer people rarely use a small word or an understandable phrase when a difficult word or an acronym will do just as nicely and confuse more people!

Access provides several layers of helpful on-line advice. Therefore, you don't have to refer to your Access manuals all the time if you need to look for an answer. Access provides *context-sensitive help*, which gives you helpful advice on whatever you're doing at the time you request help.

Access also provides *AccessWizards,* which can guide you step-by-step through the design and creation of a form or report. You'll learn more about AccessWizards throughout this book.

Skip This, It's Technical

The concepts behind relational database systems were solidified in the early 1970s by Dr. E. F. Codd of the IBM Research Laboratory in San Jose. Dr. Codd designed the relational database theory that programs such as Access attempt to adhere to. Although some argue that a true RDBMS as Dr. Codd proposed does not yet exist, the storage of data values in one place, with different views of that data being available, is one primary block in the relational database foundation.

Still Confused?

If you don't yet feel that you are a database expert, relax. The bottom line is this: if you have to work with a bunch of data, in virtually any format, for any reason, Access can help you manage that data. Access has a colorful and easy-to-use graphical interface that enables you to describe your data, enter it, change it, and report it in many different ways.

The best way to begin learning about Access is to take a short detour into database design, starting in the next chapter. Semester-long college courses and complete tomes have been written on database design, but beginners don't have to be experts to begin making Access work for them.

Fun Fact
Before disk drives became plentiful, database files were stored on big computer tapes. Unlike today, when data can be retrieved in a split second, data retrieval sometimes took several hours. We've come a long way!

The next chapter provides some guidelines that begin shaping your approach to data and Access. Access allows easy changing of your original database design. When you make some mistakes the first few times you design an Access database, you'll see how easy mistakes are to correct.

YIKES!

If you're new to computers, it helps to have had some introduction to them. *The Complete Idiot's Guide to PCs* (Alpha Books, 1993) is an excellent book for beginning computer users, and it goes into much more detail than this book does.

Chapter Wrap-Up

This chapter packed you up for your Access journey. You now know the difference between data and information, and you have some idea of what Access can do. Nevertheless, you have about 24 chapters to go before feeling as if you understand all that you should. Enjoy your tour of Access.

Diving In

● Understand that Access is a friendly graphical database program that enables you to organize and report your data so that the data is meaningful and not a bunch of unorganized facts and figures.

Sunk

- Don't be afraid to try using Access. If you're new to database programs, remember that you don't have to be an Access expert to begin using Access right away. Access makes changing your mind easier than most other database programs do.

2

Where Do I Begin?

Put Design in Your Data

- Getting a Grip on Databases 14
- Breaking the Database into Tables 16
- The Format of Tables 17
- The Key to Understanding 19
- What Now? 21

Whether you realize it or not, the data you work with often relates in some way and has structure. Before putting data into Access, you must first spend time analyzing your database needs and putting your data into some kind of structure.

The purpose of this chapter is to give you an idea of the up-front work required before you use Access. Don't let the term *work* frighten you! Access saves you effort and makes your work easier. Before using Access, however, you need to learn the preliminary database concepts that this chapter discusses.

There are several ways to approach learning Access. Most agree that you must learn the structure of Access data before going to the keyboard and using Access. Most disagree, however, on the method needed to teach the structure of Access data. You have to learn new terms such as *database, table, records,* and *fields.* Instead of learning dry dictionary explanations such as "A table is a logical grouping of related data," let's take a short detour and make some analogies to what you already know.

Getting a Grip on Databases

Suppose you kept your family's financial records in a filing cabinet. Everything related to your family's finances is in that cabinet, including insurance records, income records, expense records, checking account statements, savings and loan statements, and so forth. The entire filing cabinet could be considered your financial database. A database is a collection of data values that go together.

PSST! Not all of a database's values have pure relationships with each other. That is, the insurance records in the filing cabinet (database) don't directly relate to your loan records, although both are part of your family's financial records.

HMM... If you took classes at your local college and received grade reports each semester, your grades would *not* be part of your financial database. If you put your grades in one of the filing cabinet drawers, you would have two databases in the cabinet. (Your tuition payment receipt would be part of the financial records, but your grades wouldn't be.)

Here's what we have so far: a filing cabinet with a database consisting of your family's financial records. Not all of that data relates, but it all falls within the overall category of your family's financial records. Figure 2.1 shows your view of a database at this point.

Figure 2.1.

A database is like a filing cabinet drawer with related data.

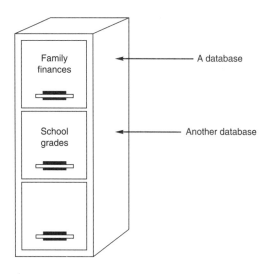

Breaking the Database into Tables

If you threw all your family's financial records into the filing cabinet without organizing them, you'd have a mess! Therefore, you would first get a bunch of file folders and divide the data into separate files within the cabinet. You would put all your checking account statements and checkbook registers in one file folder, your insurance information in another folder, and so on.

As with the filing cabinet, you can't throw all your data into a database without breaking the data into separate groups called *tables.* A table is analogous to file folders in your filing cabinet. Therefore, if you wanted to organize your family's finances using Access, you would create a database to hold everything and then segment the data into several tables that would hold related data.

YIKES!

At first, knowing how to divide massive data into tables isn't always easy. It takes practice. Because a table holds related data, you wouldn't put your insurance receipt into your income file folder. If you did, your files would lose all integrity and you'd be back to a mix-up of data thrown together without organization. Figure 2.2 shows you how a table relates to a database.

PSST!  Many times, file folders relate to each other. For example, you would pay an insurance bill with a check, and the check number might tie the two together. You'd deposit your paycheck in your savings or checking account, and the transaction would be related to the date of deposit. You'll find that you can connect two Access tables that have something in common so that Access can report from both tables at once.

Figure 2.2.

Database tables hold related data, as do file folders in a filing cabinet.

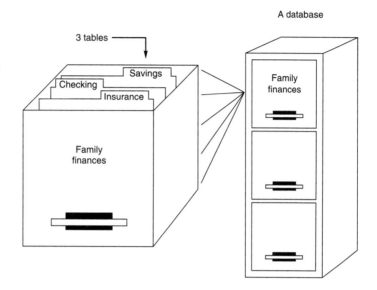

The Format of Tables

A computer needs to have a little more structure than the human mind (well, more than *most* human minds!). Access allows a little more freedom with its data than many database programs, but you still must be able to break your tables into rows and columns of data. A row in a table is called a *record*, and a column is called a *field*.

A checkbook register is a perfect example of records and fields. The records are the lines on which you record checks written and deposits made. The fields would be the columns for the check number, the date, the description, the amount, and the balance. Figure 2.3 shows how a table can be broken down into records and fields.

Figure 2.3.

*Records are rows,
and fields are
columns in a
table.*

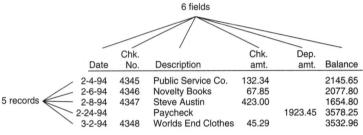

	Chk. No.	Description	Chk. amt.	Dep. amt.	Balance
2-4-94	4345	Public Service Co.	132.34		2145.65
2-6-94	4346	Novelty Books	67.85		2077.80
2-8-94	4347	Steve Austin	423.00		1654.80
2-24-94		Paycheck		1923.45	3578.25
3-2-94	4348	Worlds End Clothes	45.29		3532.96

HMM...

Like the checkbook register, a table's fields vary as to the type of data they hold. Some fields hold only numbers, some fields hold words, and some fields hold a combination of letters and numbers, such as an address field in a name-and-address table.

Skip This, It's Technical

Access allows for a *memo* field, which you'll read more about a little later. Memo fields can be extremely long, sometimes holding many paragraphs of data. If you store a lot of data, such as an insurance payment's coverage terms, in a memo field, that field will span several rows in the field. Each of these rows is not a different record, because they reside within a field. Records are always collections of one or more fields, not rows within a single long field.

PSST!

When two tables relate through a common field (or a group of fields), Access doesn't duplicate the data in both tables, even though it seems that the same data appears in two different places. Access is *relational,* which means that the

data appears only once in the entire database. When you break a database into several different tables, Access actually divides only the *view* of the data into tables. The data itself is stored only once.

Skip This, It's Technical

Access uses *data pointers* to keep track of overlapping data between tables instead of duplicating the data in more than one place. The use of pointers reduces the memory requirements of your database and ensures the data's integrity.

The Key to Understanding

Have you ever gotten mad at your credit card or utility company because they treat you like a number? When you call to complain about something, before they will even listen to you, they want that 300-digit customer number that they've given you. Perhaps after reading this section, you won't be so quick to feel nameless.

Companies computerize to save money and promote efficiency, and hopefully you as a consumer benefit through lower bills. Computers, unlike people, don't distinguish between names very well. For instance, if someone enters your name in a computer as St. John, and someone else comes along and looks you up by typing either Saint John or ST John, the computer will *not* find a match! You know the names are the same, but to a mindless machine, the abbreviation and extra period are part of the original name. Computers can easily distinguish between numbers, however. Therefore, companies assign unique numbers to every individual so that even two people with the same name can be distinguished.

When you design a table, you need to supply a field that is unique throughout all the records. If you were creating a table of people, a good field choice would be their Social Security numbers, because everybody has a different one. A checkbook register would have check numbers that identify each field. Access calls this field a *primary key* field.

Sometimes, two or more fields have to be taken together as one to form a primary key field. A local video store might keep track of its customers through telephone numbers. Each tape rental might be made by a different member of the household. Therefore, when a customer rents a tape, that customer's first name is merged to the end of the telephone number to create a unique field for the rental records of the day.

If a table has a field that isn't unique, Access offers to create a unique field for you. The Access-created primary key field will consist of sequential numbers, beginning with 1, that are automatically inserted into every record as you enter data. It is possible to keep a table from having a specified primary key field, but this is not recommended. If your data doesn't contain a field (or a combination of fields) that can be specified uniquely as a primary key, let Access add the sequential number field for you.

Database key fields are the primary reason every product in the U.S. has a unique bar code, every person has a unique Social Security number, and every customer has a different account number. Maybe being "just a number" isn't such a bad idea if it means more accuracy and lower costs to us in the long run.

Check the box that your copy of Access came in. The concept of a key is so important to Access that the Access logo is a key!

What Now?

Now that you've got some terms behind you, you might be wondering where Access fits in. Once you've organized your data to fit the database-table-record-field structures, Access is then free to analyze, fetch, store, change, and print that data any way you want. Access does this very quickly—much quicker than you can organize records using a filing cabinet.

HMM... Suppose that a university wanted to send a special course mailing to its female business majors between the ages of 18 and 45 who live within the university's ZIP code. Without computers, such a list would take several people several hours to compile. If information about the student population is in an Access database, Access will not only compile the list, but also begin printing the mailing labels in alphabetical order within a couple of seconds!

Chapter Wrap-Up

You now have some terms under your belt to help you get started running Access. The terms *database*, *table*, *record*, and *field* are part of the database developer's language. Without an understanding of these terms, you'd be lost before you even began.

Relating these terms to filing cabinet files helps database new-comers get accustomed to the concepts. If you make a $75 payment to the electric company in March and an $83 payment in April, both check stubs and utility receipts would go in the same file folder. If you were using Access, the checks would be two records in your utility payment table.

A database is your whole collection of data, a table is a subset of that database, a record is a row in the table, and a field is a column in the table. After a few more chapters, you won't even have to think about the differences between these words.

Diving In

- Use Access to keep track of your data in a database, just as you would use a filing cabinet to hold files that go together.

- Break your database into separate tables, and have each table hold related data.

- You'll get more comfortable knowing which kinds of data go together as you see more database examples throughout this book. For a while, this book works with a single table until you understand the funda-mentals of Access, and then more tables are added to the database.

- When designing a database table, determine a field that uniquely identifies every record in the table. That field will be the table's primary key. If the data does not lend itself to a unique field, Access will supply a primary key for you.

Fun Fact

You might recall from Chapter 1, "What's Access All About?" that the man who best defined relational database theory was Dr. E. F. Codd. Dr. Codd's relational theory requires a unique key for each record, and Access is more than happy to oblige. It is said that each field in each table's record must be related to the key, the entire key, and nothing but the key, so help you Codd.

Sunk

- Don't stick all your data in one big table, because that's as bad as throwing all your financial records in one big box and opening the box the day before your taxes are due. (That would be stupid. I should know; I do it all the time!)

- Don't use a text field, such as a person's name, for a primary key. Names overlap, and different people can enter the same person's name different ways.

How Do I Install Access?

Access Installs Itself

● *Installing Access* 26
● *Starting and Stopping Access* 29

Access is easy to install because Windows and Access do all the work. If Access is already on your computer, you can skip to the section titled "Starting and Stopping Access" later in this chapter.

Installing Access means that you have to copy the Access program to your computer's hard disk from all the diskettes that came with your Access package. Figure 3.1 shows an Access user before installing Access. Things look sad, but it doesn't take long to get Access in the computer. The first part of this chapter shows you how.

Figure 3.1.

Without Access on your computer's hard disk, you might as well use a filing cabinet for your data.

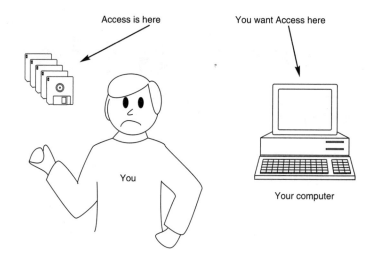

Access is here

You want Access here

You

Your computer

Installing Access

Access is a powerful program, but with that power comes a computer requirement that is more stringent than most PC programs need. Access requires that your computer meet or exceed the following hardware specifications:

- An IBM-compatible 80386 processor or higher.

- A hard disk with at least 13 megabytes (MB) of space free.

- An EGA or a VGA (or higher) display monitor and video adapter card.

- Two or more MB of internal random-access memory (RAM). At least 4MB is recommended.

- A Windows-compatible mouse, trackball, or other mouse-like pointing device.

- MS-DOS or PC-DOS 3.1 or later (5.0 or later is recommended).

- Windows 3.0 or later (3.1 or later is recommended).

YIKES!

If you are new to computers and are unfamiliar with all these terms, it won't hurt anything to try installing Access and see what happens. Access won't install to a computer with too few resources. Just be sure to find out whether your computer has Windows and a mouse already installed before you begin, because they are must-haves for installing Access.

PSST! Unlike some Windows programs, Access really does require a mouse. Most Windows programs take advantage of a mouse but also enable you to use the keyboard if you prefer. Access is one of those programs for which both the keyboard and a mouse are required.

Start Microsoft Windows if it isn't already started on your computer. Usually, this means typing `win` at the DOS prompt. Make sure the words *Program Manager* appear at the top of the screen. If these words don't appear, you might have to get help finding out how to start Program Manager on your machine.

In your Access package, you'll find several diskettes. Find the one labeled *Disk 1*, and put it in one of the diskette drive slots. Some people have more than one diskette drive. If your disk drive named A: is the right size, use it; otherwise, use B:.

Select the File menu by clicking with the mouse pointer on the word File in the menu at the top of the screen or by pressing Alt-F on the keyboard. The File menu appears. Select Run to display the Run dialog box, and type the following text in the Command Line text box:

```
a:setup
```

 **PSST!**

If you put the Access diskette in drive B:, change the a: to b:. Program Manager doesn't care whether you use uppercase or lowercase letters.

Press Enter. After a brief pause, the Access installation program asks you a few questions about your name and your company's name. Then Access gets to work installing itself on your computer. Now you are on your way to installing Access, but the installation will take a while. You have to wait at your computer throughout the installation because Access needs answers to some questions, and you have to swap diskettes when the installation program tells you to.

HMM...

The Access installation program is intelligent, and it will determine a lot about your computer. If you don't know the answer to a question asked during installation, often you can press Enter to accept the *default* answer. Default answers are answers that Access guesses at if you don't tell it differently.

YIKES!

If you have a networked computer and know nothing about the network, here's a word of advice: Yell for help! Because Access requires some information about your specific network, you might have to track down your *Network Administrator* (that's computer talk for *Network Head Honcho*) to describe your network's hardware to Access.

The installation program asks you which type of installation you want—Complete, Custom, or Minimum. Select the Complete installation option. If you don't, you'll have to make a lot of decisions about Access that you probably don't want to make at this time. As long as you have enough free disk space (13MB), selecting the Complete option ensures that you'll have everything you need, and the installation program won't bother you with a lot of petty questions.

When Access finishes the entire installation procedure, you see a new program group window on your screen similar to the one in Figure 3.2. The most important icon in the window is the one with the key labeled "Microsoft Access." That's the icon you use to start the Access database program.

Starting and Stopping Access

Starting Access is easy. If the words *Microsoft Access* under the Access icon are highlighted, you only have to press the Enter key. Otherwise, double-click the mouse pointer on the Access icon, and Access will start.

Figure 3.2.

*The newly
installed Access
program group.*

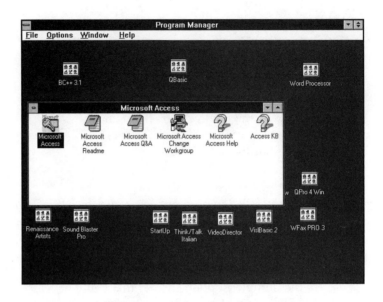

YIKES!

Get ready to tour some strange screens. Even though
Access and Windows are easy to use, they take some
getting used to. Sometimes, several different windows and
menus might be displayed on the screen as you run Access.
Keeping them straight isn't always easy, even for the Access pros!

After a brief pause, indicated by an hourglass cursor, you see the
Access copyright window, followed by the Access opening title
screen, shown in Figure 3.3. This screen is called the *startup window.*
From the startup window, you can do one of four things. For now,
don't do anything unless you want to explore a bit on your own.

Figure 3.3.

The Access startup window.

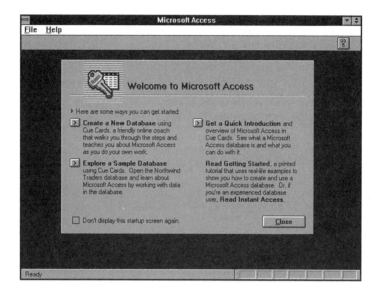

PSST! It's fine if you want to take off and play around with Access. If you decide to explore the sample database (by clicking the second choice in the startup window), don't change any data or add any data to the sample database. You'll want the data intact in case you later go through the Access reference manuals and follow their examples.

YIKES!

Before going much further, you should learn how to quit Access. Although you can turn off your computer before quitting Access, you shouldn't do so. You could lose data in your database.

If the startup window is still on the screen, click the Close button in the lower-right portion of the startup window or press Alt-C, and the startup window will go away.

To quit Access, select File from the menu at the top of the screen (by clicking File or by pressing Alt-F on the keyboard), then select Exit from the menu. Doing so ensures that your database is safely tucked away on the disk.

Chapter Wrap-Up

Before you use Access, you must install it. Installing Access requires little more than typing `setup` and inserting diskettes. Once Access is installed, start it by double-clicking its Windows program icon. Exit from Access when you're done by selecting FileExit from the menu.

Diving In

- Install Access on your computer's hard disk.

- Start Access by opening the Microsoft Access program group and double-clicking the Microsoft Access icon.

Sunk

- Don't turn off your computer without exiting Access. You might lose some data if you don't properly exit to Windows when you're finished with Access.

How Can I Get Help?

Check Out Help and Cue Cards

- Help Is a Keystroke Away 34
- Getting More Help 37
- Searching for Help 38
- Context-Sensitive Help 39
- Cue Cards Extend Help 40
- Magic Wizards 41

Access gives you help all along the way. As with most Windows programs, Access provides helpful on-line advice whenever you need it. Although the on-line help doesn't go into great detail on table design and so forth, it's useful for finding out all the options that are available at the time you're trying something.

The Access help system also provides a series of *cue cards* that walk you through the generation of tables, reports, forms, and many other objects in Access. This chapter shows you a little about the cue cards.

YIKES!

Despite Microsoft's best efforts, the cue cards often confuse beginners more than help them. The cue cards are pop-up windows that appear on your Access screen when you want them. The problem with the cue card windows is that they often get in the way by covering up something you need to see.

Help Is a Keystroke Away

There are several ways to get help with Access. Often there is more than one way to get the same help on a topic. Don't feel as though you have to master the entire help system before you begin. You'll be surprised at how much you use the help system for the little things but rarely use it for the big questions. You'll refer to this book a lot when beginning, and then to your Access reference manuals when you're more familiar with Access.

 HMM... Despite the excellent on-line help that Access provides, you'll often like the feel and familiarity of a book like this one or your reference manuals when

you have a question. Even technically competent people such as you like the feel of books!

Start Access if it isn't already started. Get rid of the startup window by clicking the Close button. You'll be left with a blank screen with two menus at the top of the screen and a question mark button in the upper-right corner.

Skip This, It's Technical

The question mark button in the upper-right portion of the screen rests on the Access *toolbar*. As you create and manage databases with Access, more tools will appear on the toolbar, along with the question mark. If you've used another Windows product, such as Microsoft Word for Windows, you've probably seen and used toolbars before. Unlike with programs such as Word, the Access tools appear only when they're relevant to your current task. In other words, because you aren't designing a database table right at this moment, you don't see the database design tool on the toolbar.

Click the question mark tool, and the Access Help screen appears (see Figure 4.1). If you've seen a Windows-based help screen before, this Access help screen will seem familiar because Access uses the Windows help *engine* (a program that lets Windows-based programs use a common help interface).

To get rid of any help window, you can select File Exit. A quicker way is to double-click the help window's *control-menu button,* shown in Figure 4.2.

Figure 4.1.

Requesting help after clicking the help tool on the toolbar.

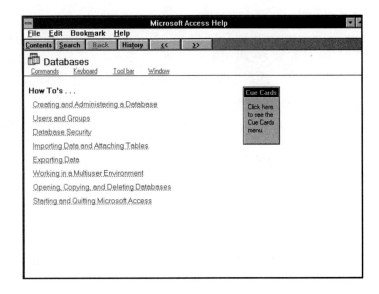

Figure 4.2.

The control-menu button.

PSST! Double-clicking *any* window's control-menu button closes that window. You might want to remember this shortcut to exit Windows programs more quickly than by using the keyboard.

After closing the help window, press F1. *Voilà!* The same help window appears that appeared when you clicked the help tool earlier. The F1 key is the shortcut key to display this help screen. Again, there are several ways to achieve the same goal when using the built-in help system.

Getting More Help

With the help screen still displayed, choose Contents by clicking with the mouse pointer or by pressing Alt-C. This screen is really a better place to begin looking for help than the previous help screen was. You can go directly to this screen by selecting Help Contents from the Access menu at the top of the screen instead of clicking the question mark tool if you want to save a step.

Move the mouse pointer around the screen. As you do, you'll notice that it changes to a hand shape. The hand indicates that the mouse pointer is covering a cross-reference of some kind inside the help system. If you click while the mouse pointer is in the shape of a hand, you get a help screen on the topic under the hand. You can continue narrowing your help searches as many times as you like through cross-referencing.

HMM... Move the mouse pointer over Queries and click. You'll get help on Access queries. Now select the Back button at the top of the help screen, and you'll be back to where you were before you selected the Queries cross-reference. As you progress through help screens, Access keeps track of where you've been so you can backtrack if you want to.

It sometimes seems as if Access provides more help than you'll *ever* need! Click three or four cross-references (remember that a cross-reference appears whenever the mouse pointer changes to the shape of a hand). Now select the History button at the top of the help screen. Access displays a scrolling dialog box like the one in Figure 4.3.

Figure 4.3.

The History list of help topics you've traversed.

The Windows Help History box is a list of the past several topics you've requested help with (through cross-references). You can go back to any topic in the list with a click of the mouse. You can get rid of the history by double-clicking its control-menu box.

YIKES!

You're learning a lot about getting help, and you don't even know enough about Access to know what you need help on! Hang tight. You'll be glad you saw the many ways to get help so that when you need help you can get it.

Searching for Help

At any point during your Access session, you can search for a help topic by selecting from a list of available topics. Choose Search from either the Access Help menu or any of the help windows you happen to be in. Access displays the search dialog box, shown in Figure 4.4.

As with most Windows-based help search boxes, you can type the first few letters of the topic you need help with or select from the scrolling list of general topics in the center of the box.

Figure 4.4.

The Search dialog box.

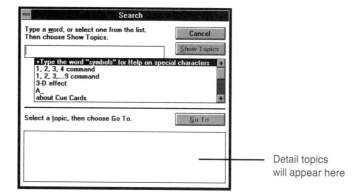

Detail topics will appear here

The bottom of the help search box is the topic section, which shows detailed topics related to the general search topics above it. For example, if you selected database window from the scrolling list of general help subjects, then clicked the Show Topics button, Access would display three specific topics related to database windows at the bottom of the box. In a way, you give Access the general subject, database window, and Access provides a more specific list of related subjects in the topic section at the bottom.

Once you select a specific topic, click the Go To button, and help will be at hand.

Context-Sensitive Help

Another way to get help is to let Access tell you what you need help with. Whenever you press F1, Access looks at whatever command, object, or menu you are currently using and offers helpful advice on that subject.

YIKES!

Don't be alarmed if you want help and press F1 only to find that Access doesn't offer any help on that topic.

Access doesn't offer context-sensitive help on *every* topic, only on some. It's easy enough to search for the topic you need help on (using the methods discussed in the preceding section) if the context-sensitive help doesn't give you what you need.

Cue Cards Extend Help

Fun Fact
Before computer programs began offering on-line help, you had to keep countless reference manuals beside your computer. How frustrating it must have been for the ancient computer users to have to leave the keyboard and look something up by hand!

The *cue cards* in Access work like a progressive, step-by-step help system. Instead of making you select the next topic, the cue cards offer help screens that walk you through an entire procedure, such as creating a table.

The beauty of cue cards sometimes is their downfall as well. The cue cards stay as the top window *while* you follow their directions. For example, if you wanted to view the cue cards for creating a table, you could create the table while following the cue cards' advice. When you were done with one Cue Card, you could go on to the next and follow its cues. However, cue cards often hide some object on the screen that you need to see or work with. Unlike with the regular help windows, you can't resize or move the Cue Card screens. Beginners often become frustrated with the cue cards and rely on their own ability and the regular help screens.

If you want to walk through a Cue Card session, press F1 on the help screen and click the Cue Card box.

You'll see a list of Cue Card topics from which you can choose. The last one in the list (I'm Not Sure) is a good start for newcomers. (However, this book is even better, and it doesn't hide important parts of your screen!)

Magic Wizards

Access provides one more helpful technique that this book teaches starting in Chapter 12, "What Is a Form?" *AccessWizards* are guiding hands (well, dialog boxes) that lead you step-by-step through the creation of a form or report. Unlike cue cards that tell you what to do, AccessWizards lead you through the creation of a form or report and actually create the form or report for you as you answer questions.

Chapter Wrap-Up

Access utilizes the integrated Windows help system thoroughly. Help is always at your fingertips if you click the question mark help tool, press F1, or select from the pull-down menu. The help system provides cross-references, context-sensitive help, and even cue cards that walk you through the creation of a database.

Practice a little by clicking the help tool and looking around. Walk through a cue card session if you like by clicking the cue card icon or by selecting Cue Cards from the Help menu.

With all the ready-to-help features that Access and this book provide, you'll never be stuck wondering what to do next!

Diving In

- Before jumping into your first database, get acquainted with the on-line help system. You'll never leave home without it!

- Press F1 or choose the help tool (the question mark on the right side of the tool bar) to get a help screen. Depending on what you're doing, Access may or may not offer context-sensitive help on the very operation you're performing. If not, you can easily search for the help you need.

- Use the Back and History help buttons to repeat help topics you've seen previously and want to return to.

Sunk

- Don't rely a lot on the cue cards when you first begin. Although they can be helpful, they cover up a lot of your working screens. It helps to become familiar with Access before relying too heavily on the cue cards.

Part II
Getting Acquainted with Access

What Do I Do First?

Create a Database and Learn the Tools

- *Filing Your Database* 46
- *This Book's Sample Database* 47
- *Creating the Database File* 48
- *The Database Window* 50
- *Looking Around* 55

You're ready to begin! Now that you understand a few preliminary database concepts, have Access installed, and know where to go for help if you need it, you're ready to get the ball rolling toward creating a database of your own.

In this chapter, you'll see how to create a database from scratch. Throughout this book, you'll create and add to a sample database. You'll learn the process needed to move from the early database-creation stages to the reporting of the data once the database is complete. This book's sample database isn't exactly the same database you'll need, but it mirrors the design problems, database-creation steps, and implementation details you'll face.

If you have an immediate need for a database, don't create this book's specific database, but create your own as you follow the book. You'll find that you follow the same steps the book illustrates for most databases you'll create.

A good carpenter knows the best carpentry tools, and a good database designer knows the best database tools for the job. This chapter introduces you to the six primary tools used in Access.

Filing Your Database

One of the drawbacks that most database products suffer from is the glut of files needed for each individual database application. For example, you might need a small database to run a small mailing list with names and addresses. Lots of Access's competitors might create three or more files just to store all the data in a single database. The files exist because their parent database product stores the table relationships in one file, the data in another, the database structure in another, and the reports and forms in several more.

Access stores everything it needs for each individual database in a single file on disk. Although this file can become large, you have to do much less bookkeeping when you want to copy, move, or delete a database. To copy your database application from your home computer to your office computer, you only have to copy one file to a diskette and take it with you (assuming that the diskette is large enough to hold the file).

HMM... All the related pieces of an Access database are called *objects*. For instance, a table is an object. The database data, however, is not an object. Only Access items that work with data are objects.

PSST! All database filenames end in the .MDB extension (for *Microsoft DataBase*). When you create a database, you don't have to specify the .MDB extension because Access supplies it for you.

This Book's Sample Database

Throughout this book, you'll see a sample database created for *Laura Landlady's Rental Properties*. Before this book is finished, you will have created several tables, forms, queries, and reports that help Laura keep her records straight. The format of Laura's database application probably will be similar to the first database you want to create.

YIKES!

Even though Access is relatively easy to learn, it is still a comprehensive tool with many pieces. Your first database should be relatively simple. (You can always add to it later.) Please don't jump off the deep end and create a budget for the world's economy your first time at bat! The concepts of Access take a while to sink in.

Creating the Database File

A database might have one table or 100 tables. No matter how complex your database will be, the first step is to create it. Here's how you do it:

1. Display the File pull-down menu.

2. Select New Database.... The New Database window, shown in Figure 5.1, appears.

3. Access offers you a database name, db1.mdb, but that's not a good name because it's not meaningful to your application. To create the sample rental property application in this book, type the following name at the File Name prompt:

    RENTALS

    As with any DOS filename, you can type the name in upper-case or lowercase letters. Remember that Access adds the .MDB extension, so you don't have to.

Figure 5.1.

Getting ready to specify a new database.

Type the new database name here.

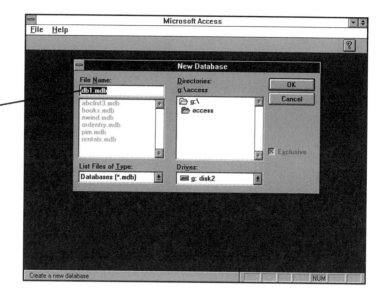

PSST!   If you want, you can select a drive or directory other than the one chosen by Access. Simply select from the Directories or the Drives list, or type the complete drive and pathname before the database name. For this example, use the default drive and directory unless there's a good reason to do otherwise (for example, if you're running low on disk space on the drive that Access uses).

4.   Press Enter after specifying the filename. When you do, you'll see a box called the *database window,* like the one shown in Figure 5.2.

Figure 5.2.

*The database
window is the
control center for
the rest of Access.*

HMM...   Once the database is created, you'll see that some
tools have been added to the toolbar next to the help
question mark. There are more tools because you can
do more things now.

PSST!   Access filenames aren't limited to 8 characters, except for the
name of your original database file. All tables, forms, and
reports can have names much longer than 8 characters.
Access provides an interface that enables you to keep track
of your Access objects using names as long as 64 characters.

The Database Window

The database window is the control center for maneuvering through
your whole database application. Right now, the window is bare.
Other than the six icons on the left and the three buttons at the top,
not much is there. But there shouldn't be! You haven't added
anything to the database yet because you only just created it.

HMM... The six icons represent six of Access's most common *objects*. An object is a part of your database (not the data itself), such as a table or a report. Some people refer to these six icons as *tools*.

Each of the next sections describes these six objects. Don't feel as though you have to master them now. You should, however, get acquainted with the terms and behaviors within the database window.

PSST! Here's a tip that will enlarge the size of the database window: Put the mouse pointer over the database window title bar that reads Database: RENTALS, and double-click. The database window will increase to fill the full screen. Once you've added several tables to the database, enlarging the window lets you see more tables at once. To put the window back to its original smaller size, click the restore button (in the upper-right corner of the window), shown in Figure 5.3.

Figure 5.3.
The restore button.

The Table Object

Click the Table button. At the top of the database window, you'll see three buttons labeled New, Open, and Design. (The last two are grayed out. There is no table to open or design because you just created the database and haven't created tables for it.) As you create tables for the database, you'll see new table names being added to this database window's list of tables in the white area to the right of the objects.

The buttons at the top of the database window change when you change objects. For instance, click the Report object, and you'll see a different set of buttons. Now, click Table to get back to where you were.

Recall from Chapter 2, "Where Do I Begin?" that a table is a set of related data, with a primary key that uniquely identifies each record in the table. The first step toward completing a database application is to create a table structure that can hold your database data. You'll do this in the next chapter.

YIKES!

If you don't create tables, your databases will have no structure, and there will be no place to store data.

The Query Object

A *query* is nothing more than a question about your data. You define queries, and Access remembers them and produces up-to-date answers when you select the query. A query might be a question such as "How many people paid on time last month?" or "How much have we spent on advertising this fiscal year?" Queries enable you to pull summary information from a large database and select only the data you want to look at.

HMM... You can't ask Access a question directly because Access doesn't understand English! However, Access *is* visual. In Chapter 16, "What Is a Query?" you'll learn how to use the mouse and keyboard to create queries that answer questions.

You must query a table (or a group of tables) before you can do anything with a subset of data from a table. Unless you pull the data out of a table via a query, you have nothing to look at or print.

You can use queries to change data. You might need to change only the records in your database that match a certain criterion, and you can specify that criterion with a query.

PSST! Access provides *query by example* (QBE) that enables you to create a query with the guided help of Access. Therefore, even though you can't ask questions in English, Access helps you design your queries so that it can understand exactly what information you need. QBE is discussed in more detail in Chapter 18, "How Do Queries Work with Forms?"

The Form Object

Figure 5.4 shows what a form looks like. Forms are easy to work with because they look like the paper forms you fill out for job interviews and insurance claims. You can add or change data on a form. Access gives you total freedom to design forms that look and behave exactly the way you want them to.

Figure 5.4.

Forms enable you to add and change data in your database.

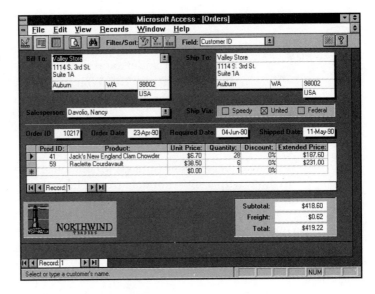

The Report Object

A report object is a printed report of your data. You can create customized reports that present your data in any manner, or you can take the default reports that Access supplies, which look pretty good and don't need any modifications.

You use a report whenever you want Access to present data on paper. That means that a report can be a month-end sales summary, mailing labels, or checks, for example.

With Access, you can view your reports on the screen before you print them. Not only do you save paper, but the report preview enables you to fine-tune reports during the design stage because you can see how a report will look as you create it instead of after you have printed it.

The Macro and Module Objects

Macros and modules are the automation tools of Access. A *macro* is a list of things you want Access to do for you, such as opening a database and printing mailing labels. You can tie a macro to a push-button you create so that Access will perform a series of actions at the push of a button instead of making you go through each action step-by-step at the keyboard.

PSST!   An Access macro is similar to some of the macros you might have used in spreadsheets or word processors. Although Access macros are not of the usual variety that record your keystrokes, Access macros are lists of common tasks you want done, such as viewing table data and printing reports.

A *module* is the way to program Access using Access Basic, a built-in programming language that is similar to the QBasic and Visual Basic programming languages.

This book doesn't cover modules because it takes too much time to teach programming concepts and because this book isn't geared toward advanced "power users" who might want to write programs. Don't fret, however, because Access is designed to meet most or all of your database needs without your having to write programs to do what you want.

Looking Around

To get an idea of what the database window looks like with lots of data in the system, load the NWIND.MDB database that comes with Access by choosing File Open Database... and selecting the file labeled `nwind.mdb`. You'll see a database window full of tables, reports, and other things. Enlarge the database window to full screen to see more table names at one time. When you're done looking at the database window, close it by choosing File Close Database. Then you can exit Access or move on to the next chapter in this book.

Chapter Wrap-Up

This chapter explained the six Access objects: tables, queries, forms, reports, macros, and modules. The database window is the starting point and control center for everything you want to do in Access. The database window launches you into any of the six objects with the click of a button.

Now that you've been introduced to the generalities of Access, it's time to get into specifics. The next chapter teaches you to build your first database.

Diving In

- Create a database file to hold your application's tables, forms, reports, queries, and modules.

- Increase the size of the database window if you want a full-screen view. (You can do this with any open window in Access.)

- When you're designing your database, think ahead about the forms and reports you'll want to see. Forms are the interactive data-entry screens in Access that enable you to look at and change data. Reports are the resulting printed data that comes from your database.

- If you need to automate tasks, you can use macros. They let someone who doesn't know Access use the database that you or some other Access developer created. You also might want to write macros for yourself to save keystrokes when you need to perform repetitive tasks.

Sunk

- Don't feel as though you have to master Access Basic any time soon. Access provides incredible power without requiring that you learn to program.

6

How Do I Create Tables?

Use the Table Object's Button

- *Creating the Table Structure*   61
- *A Word on Field Characteristics*   62
- *A Hands-On Table Structure Definition*   66

Remember that a table is one of several divisions in your database that holds related data in record and field format. Although all the data in a database is related, a table's data is specifically grouped. For example, in the sample database created in this book, Laura Landlady develops a database for her rental properties. Although her tenant data and property data should be included in the database, her tenant information (name, phone number, and so on) wouldn't be included in the same table as her property information (address, date bought, price paid, and so on).

You might think of tables as structures that hold the database's data. If your database were one gigantic table, it would be extremely difficult to find answers, and it also would be slow and inefficient.

This chapter leads you through the creation of your first table in the RENTALS database. The next chapter continues this subject by showing you how to add field characteristics to your table. The rest of this book works with this table, showing you how to enter and manipulate data in the table. Starting in Chapter 19, "How Do I Add More Tables?" you'll also add tables to the database so that you can learn how to pull data from more than one table at a time.

HMM...   In a way, the preceding chapter "built" the filing cabinet. Chapter 5, "What Do I Do First?" taught you how to create the RENTALS database for Laura Landlady's records. This chapter shows you how to create the first file folder to go in that cabinet. The file folder will hold tenant data.

Creating the Table Structure

Laura Landlady used to keep her property and tenant data in a spiral-bound notebook. She quickly found, however, that she needed a way to rearrange the records every time a tenant moved. She couldn't move pages within the spiral-bound notebook. Changing from the spiral-bound notebook to a three-ring notebook was her first move toward a flexible database record-keeping system. Moving to Access was the final step, and the one that is most likely to affect the way she does business.

HMM... The design and creation of a database for Laura Landlady's rental properties might seem silly to you. Your database needs might be very different from those of a rental property owner. Nevertheless, you will make the same decisions about your database that Laura makes about hers. Although your data might not match Laura's in format, your tables and forms certainly will behave like most of hers. Follow along and create this sample database as you go. When you finish a chapter with examples for Laura Landlady, follow the same steps for your own specific database.

Figure 6.1 shows how Laura used to keep each of her tenants' records. Because Access is so flexible and allows for so many kinds of data, Laura will find that she can reproduce this same tenant data in Access by creating a tenant table.

PSST! Before you can put data into a table, you must describe that table to Access. You must tell Access how many fields there will be and the kind of data each field will hold.

Figure 6.1.

Before using Access, Laura Landlady kept handwritten tenant records in a notebook.

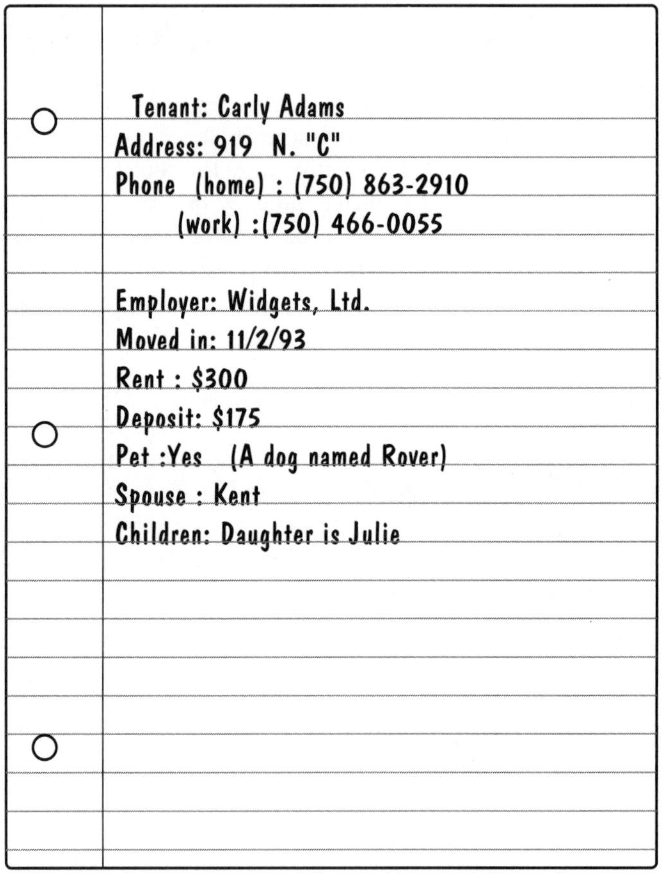

Tenant: Carly Adams
Address: 919 N. "C"
Phone (home) : (750) 863-2910
       (work) :(750) 466-0055

Employer: Widgets, Ltd.
Moved in: 11/2/93
Rent : $300
Deposit: $175
Pet :Yes   (A dog named Rover)
Spouse : Kent
Children: Daughter is Julie

A Word on Field Characteristics

Not all data has the same "look and feel." Some data, such as a dollar balance, is numeric; some, such as a person's name, is character-based; and some, such as the date due, appears in a date format. Access cares about data formats. If you ever want

to compute some kind of arithmetic quantity, for example, you must make that field numeric, not a character or a date.

Each field in an Access table can contain a different type of data. When you define the structure (the "look and feel") of a table, you are telling Access exactly what kind of data will go in each field.

Each field in an Access table has a *field name*. Field names are like the category names in Laura Landlady's handwritten table of tenant data shown in Figure 6.1. Field names enable you to refer to specific columns when you need to. Also, if you want to use the same field in two different tables, just use the same field name in both tables. Behind your back, Access stores the data in only one of the fields, but it makes you think that the data appears more than once in the database. For example, later in this book you'll see a Property ID field appear in two different tables, but Access stores them in only one location to maintain their integrity.

Table 6.1 shows you the kinds of fields that Access allows. Keep in mind that the type of fields you select for your tables depends on the kind of data you will store there. For example, you'd never store a person's name in a currency field—you'd store only monetary amounts there.

Fun Fact

With many older database programs, it was very difficult to change your mind once you created a table. Access, however, was written to be used in a dynamic environment where the format of tables might change at any time. Although planning your database ahead of time helps you focus more and develop your database quicker, if you leave something out and need to add a field later, Access lets you.

YIKES!

Don't let the wide assortment of field types worry you. You probably won't need a few of them, such as Counter and OLE Object, for a while.

Table 6.1. **The Access field data types.**

Data Type	Description
Text	Most database fields are Text. Any fields made up of one or more characters—letters, numbers, special characters (such as ?, *, (, &, #, and $), or a combination of any of these—are Text fields. The maximum length of a Text field is 255 characters. Any data that consists of numbers you won't calculate with, such as Social Security numbers, should be considered Text fields.
Memo	Memo fields can be as long as 32,000 characters and can hold the same kind of data as Text fields, only a lot more of it. Don't use a Memo field unless you want to keep notes about a record. Using Text fields for text data values is much more efficient than turning all your Text fields into Memo fields. By the way, a Memo field consumes only as much memory and disk space as the actual data requires. Even though a Memo field can be as long as 32,000 characters, it won't take that much space in memory unless your memo is actually that long.

Data Type	Description
Number	If your table contains any numeric data that you will calculate with, such as measurements and distances, you need to make the field a Number field. For money amounts, however, use the Currency data type (described later). The Currency data type is more accurate if you need to track four or fewer decimal places in your data.
Date/Time	Access can track date and time data from the year 100 to the year 9999 (but your computer probably will be obsolete by then).
Currency	Use this data type for all money amounts and for any numeric field in which accuracy to four or fewer decimal places is needed.
Counter	If you designate a Counter field, Access automatically adds one to the field when you add a new record. You can use the Counter data type to keep track of how many records are in a table.
Yes/No	If your table's records contain data that answers a yes-or-no question, designate that field as a Yes/No field. For example, you might want to know if a tenant has signed a lease or if a customer has paid a service charge.
OLE Object	Access enables you to bury pictures, spreadsheets, and even sound inside a record. The data must conform to the Windows *OLE* (*Object Linking and Embedding*) standards. You should be familiar with the usage of Windows OLE (pronounced o-LAY) objects before making a field an OLE object.

PSST! If your data doesn't have a unique field, you can add a Counter field to the table so that every record has a different count in its Counter field. As you learned in Chapter 2, "Where Do I Begin?" there are benefits for tables that contain a field with unique data values throughout every record.

A Hands-On Table Structure Definition

Start Access if it isn't already running. You need to see how to define a table structure using the information you just learned about field names and data types. Remember that you can't add data to a table until you've described each field in that table to Access. Creating a table and defining its fields is called *defining* the table.

Open the RENTALS database you created in Chapter 5: Select File Open Database..., type RENTALS, and press Enter. Access opens the database window. Guess which of the six buttons you need to use for table definition? The answer's easy: Use the Table button.

Click the Table button. Nothing much seems to happen. If another button, such as Report, were active (it wouldn't be if you just opened the database, but play along for now), clicking Table would tell Access that you were ready to work with a new or an existing table. No table names are listed in the white space next to the buttons because you have yet to add a table to this database.

HMM... The database window is your control panel to all of Access. If you need to move to a different part of Access, such as from a report definition to a structure definition, you would click the appropriate button in the database window.

You probably can guess what to do next. Click the New button. Access displays a blank table definition window like the one shown in Figure 6.2. The table definition window is nothing more than a form you fill out, telling Access what the new table will look like.

Figure 6.2.

Fill in the blanks of the table definition window to let Access know what your new table will look like.

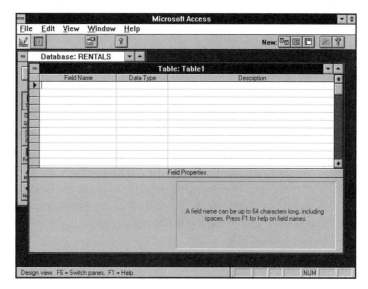

PSST!   Double-click the title bar (the one that reads Table: Table1) to enlarge the table to fill the entire screen. Although the table now covers the database window, you can move back to the database window by pressing Ctrl+F6. (Ctrl+F6 moves you between windows on the screen.) If you want to shrink the table definition window to its original size, click the window restore button in the upper-right corner of the window.

YIKES!

Despite the fact that Windows applications such as Access are touted as being easy to use, newcomers often get confused by all the overlapping windows. Think of the windows as pieces of paper on your desk. Sometimes one covers another, but you can always shift between them.

HMM...

All tables have names so that you can distinguish between them in the database. Access names your first table Table1, the second Table2, and so on (as you can tell from the title bar in the table definition window). You'll have a chance to give the table a more meaningful name in the next chapter when you save the table.

When you describe your table definition, you are working in *design view*, as opposed to *datasheet view.* Notice that the words in the lower-left corner of the screen tell you that you're in design view. In design view you create and modify the table structure. In datasheet view you enter data into an existing table.

Now you're ready to begin describing the fields in this table. The next chapter shows you how.

Chapter Wrap-Up

You now know how to create a new database table. Simply open the database, click the Table button, and select New to open the table's definition screen, called the design view.

A table is the place where your data resides. After creating a table, you're ready to partition that table into fields. How do you do that? The next chapter supplies the answers.

Diving In

- Create the first table that will hold data for your database.

- Become familiar with the different types of fields. You don't have to memorize them, because Access supplies a list you can choose from when you're ready to describe your table's fields.

- After you open the table definition window, double-click its title bar to increase the window's size to fill the entire screen. That way you can see more field descriptions at one time.

Sunk

- Don't assume that a field that will hold numeric data should be defined as type Number unless you will perform calculations of some kind with the field's values. Numeric fields that you'll only print, such as telephone numbers and numeric ID codes, should remain Text fields.

7

How Do I Describe Fields?

Use the Table Definition Window

- Describing the Fields   72
- If You Make Mistakes   76
- Specifying Other Data Types   77
- Defining More Field Properties   78
- Specifying the Primary Key   80
- Finishing the Table Definition   81

Now that you've opened the table definition window, it is time to learn how to describe the individual fields within the table. This chapter rounds out your tutorial of defining tables by showing you how to name fields and specify field characteristics. The next few chapters will work with this table, showing you how to enter and manipulate data within the table.

Without further ado, let's get to those field definitions and complete your first table in the RENTALS database.

Describing the Fields

You must tell Access what the fields in the new table will look like. As you can see from the three columns on your screen (assuming you are continuing from the preceding chapter), here at the table definition window you tell Access the name of each field, the field type, and an optional field description for the fields in the table.

PSST!  Each line in the table definition window describes another field in your file. Unless you use a super VGA graphics adapter and monitor, you will see only 16 blank lines for new fields. You can define many more than 16 fields (as many as 255 altogether) or fewer than 16. After you add the 16th field, the window scrolls down to enable you to add more fields.

A vertical cursor called the *text cursor* should be blinking in the first box under the column labeled Field Name. If it isn't, click the white Field Name box.

HMM... Remember that we are following Laura Landlady as she creates her database. The first table that Laura needs is her tenant table. When you design your own database, you have to add a table to the database before doing anything else.

Laura wants to be able to uniquely identify each tenant, and as you learned in Chapter 2, "Where Do I Begin?" a person's name is not always unique. The first field in the tenant table will hold a unique Tenant ID field. Here are the steps you should follow to define the field:

1. With the vertical text cursor resting on the first line beneath Field Name, type `Tenant ID`. You just named the first field in the tenant's table. A field name can range from 1 to 64 characters. Most Access developers capitalize the first letter in each field's word, but you can do what you want. The word *ID* looks a little funny if you don't capitalize both letters.

2. Press Tab to move the text cursor to the next column. The Enter key also moves the cursor, so use whichever key you feel most comfortable with. Most people use Tab because a corresponding Shift+Tab takes you back to the preceding column. Your screen will look like the one in Figure 7.1. Notice that Access added a minitable in the lower pane (the bottom half) of the screen. For now, ignore the table and finish entering the field definitions.

YIKES!

With only a few tenants, does Laura Landlady really need to assign each one a unique Tenant ID? Later, Laura will need to assign each tenant to a house or an apartment, and the

Tenant ID field will provide that relationship. The tenants don't have to ever know that Laura has assigned them an ID. The Tenant ID exists just to make working with the tables easier. Of course, if Laura Landlady becomes a multibillionaire owning thousands of properties, she might have to resort to telling her tenants their IDs so that she can record their rent payments faster and look up information quicker when they call with questions.

Figure 7.1.

After entering the first field's name.

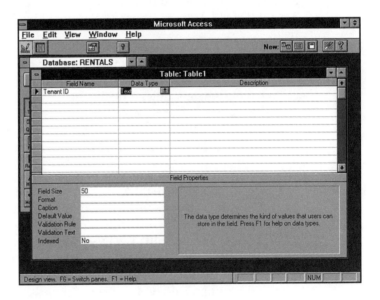

The list of field data types includes every data type described in the preceding chapter (Text, Memo, and so on). You must use one of the eight data types supplied.

3. When you move the cursor to the middle column (the Data Type column), Access automatically displays `Text`. Most fields in a table are Text fields, so Access sees no reason why you should type `Text`. The arrow next to `Text` produces a list of all the other field data types if you click the arrow with the mouse (Alt+down arrow also displays the list of data types). Click the arrow to see the field types from which you can choose. For now, leave the highlight over `Text` and press Tab to accept Text as this first field's data type.

4. The cursor now rests under the Description column. You can enter a description of up to 255 characters. For now, type the following description and then press Tab to move the cursor to the next row:

    `Uniquely identifies each tenant`

5. Continue entering the following fields in the same manner:

Field Name	Data Type	Description
Tenant's Name	Text	Last, then first separated by comma
Property ID	Text	ID of this tenant's property
Phone Number (home)	Text	Tenant's home phone number
Phone Number (work)	Text	Tenant's work phone number

When you've entered the five fields—Tenant ID through Phone Number (work)—the Table window should look like the one in Figure 7.2.

Skip This, It's Technical

In Laura Landlady's handwritten tenant records that you saw in the preceding chapter, she put the tenant's address rather than a property ID code as the previous field entry indicates.

Because the property table created later in the book will have a unique field (the primary key for that table) named Property ID, it would be a waste of time to type the full property's address when a short property ID is all that's needed to tie the tenant to the property the tenant lives in.

Figure 7.2.

After entering the first five field definitions.

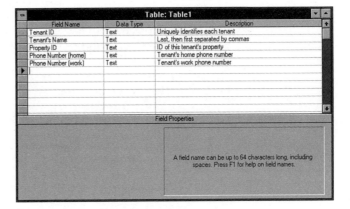

If You Make Mistakes

Access provides several ways to correct mistakes you make as you enter the field information. If you make a typing mistake and see the mistake before pressing Tab or Enter, press Backspace to erase what you've typed, and type the correct information. If the mistake appears toward the beginning of the box, use the left arrow to move the cursor left, over the characters, without erasing as you move the cursor.

The text cursor is always in *insert mode*. This means that if you move the cursor left and type in front of existing characters, those existing characters will be pushed over to the right. If you press the Insert key (sometimes labeled Ins), Access changes to *overtype mode,* in which the characters you type replace the following characters. The Insert key toggles between insert and overtype mode every time you press it.

If you've pressed Tab or Enter and you realize that you made a mistake in a previous box within the table definition window, move the mouse pointer over the error, and click the mouse button. The text cursor will appear right where you clicked the mouse, and you can then make your correction as just described.

PSST! The Delete key (sometimes labeled Del) deletes whatever character is under the text cursor and shifts all the following text over to the left.

Specifying Other Data Types

There are a few more fields to enter. Four of the fields will have a data type different from that of Text. Therefore, with the cursor under Field Name in the sixth line of the window, follow these steps to enter the remaining field definitions:

1. Type `Date Moved In` for the sixth Field Name, and press Enter.

2. Instead of accepting the Text data type, press the Alt+down arrow (or click the mouse on the box's arrow) to display the list of data type values. Highlight the Date/Time data type by pressing the down arrow key followed by Enter or by clicking the Date/Time row with the mouse.

3. Type Date moved into property for the field's description.

4. In the same manner as in the preceding three steps, enter Date Moved Out for the seventh field name, select the Date/Time data type, and enter Date moved out of property for the description.

YIKES!

As you might have guessed, current tenants will not have a Date Moved Out value when you add their data. However, Laura wants to track her former tenants as well as current tenants, so she needs to record the date that any move out.

5. There are three fields remaining to describe. Enter their values as follows:

Field Name	Data Type	Description
Rent Amount	Currency	Monthly rent
Deposit Amount	Currency	Security deposit
Pet Deposit?	Yes/No	Is there a pet?

Defining More Field Properties

The Field Name, Data Type, and Description columns are properties of each of the 10 fields you just described. There are some additional properties that you can set as well; they appear in the lower pane of the table definition window under the title Field Properties.

YIKES!

If you want to get extremely picky, Access calls those boxes in the lower pane *properties*, and the three columns above are known by their individual names, Field Name, Data Type, and Description. In reality, they are all properties of each field.

The Field Properties further describe details of the table's fields. If you left the Field Properties alone, Access would never care. If you don't do anything with the Field Properties, Access assumes default values (basically, Access guesses what the properties should be) for the properties.

Click the mouse on the row that describes the Tenant ID field, and look at the properties in the window's lower pane. Figure 7.3 shows what you see.

Figure 7.3.

The Tenant ID field property values.

Field Properties	
Field Size	50
Format	
Caption	
Default Value	
Validation Rule	A field name can be up to 64 characters long, including spaces. Press F1 for help on field names.
Validation Text	
Indexed	No

Only the first property, Field Size, and last property, Indexed, currently have values (50 and No, respectively). For a while, we'll ignore Indexed and most of the other properties. The Field Size property will be useful to change. By default, all text fields have a width of 50 characters—which means that there will be a lot of wasted space because most people's names are shorter than 25 characters.

HMM...

The properties you are viewing are specific just to Text fields. The Date/Time, Currency, and other field data types have their own sets of field properties. For example, the Date/Time fields are always the same width, so Access does not enable you to change the width of those fields.

Click each of the five Text field rows, click their corresponding Field Size properties, and enter the sizes shown here:

Field Name	Field Size
Tenant ID	10
Tenant's Name	25
Property ID	3
Phone Number (home)	14
Phone Number (work)	14

PSST!   If you want to move back and forth between the upper pane that contains the fields and the lower pane that contains each field's property, use the F6 key or click with the mouse.

As you saw, there are more properties than just Field Size that you can specify for each field. Many of these require further learning, but we'll get to them soon enough. The remaining properties describe things such as how the data should be entered and default values in case the user does not enter a new value.

Specifying the Primary Key

The Tenant ID field, which uniquely defines each record, was going to be Laura Landlady's key field. To specify the Tenant ID field as

the primary key, click the mouse pointer over the first row (for Field Name Tenant ID), and select Edit Select Primary Key. Access places a picture of a key in front of the Tenant ID field to indicate that this field is the primary key.

PSST! Remember that the primary key will be used later to search for data quickly.

HMM... If you want a primary key to be made from more than one field, select the fields that will comprise the primary key by holding down the Ctrl key while clicking the row selector (the thin column to the left of the field names) for each field you want in the key. After you've highlighted the fields, select Edit Select Primary Key. The key symbol will appear to the left of all the fields that make up the key.

Finishing the Table Definition

You've now defined your first table! The only step left is to save the table structure to the database file and tuck everything away safely to the disk. When you're ready to save anything in Access to the disk, you should display the File pull-down menu and select Save.

Unlike most other database programs that allow only 8-character table names, Access tables can have names as long as 64 characters. Type the name `Tenant Data` and press Enter. You'll see the name centered at the top of the table definition window.

YIKES!

If you do not save the table under a new name, Access assigns the name Table1 to the table. Table1 is not an invalid name, but it is not easy to remember. Give your tables descriptive names so that you'll know which table is which when you select one from a list.

Close the table definition window by pressing Ctrl+F4. (You can also click the control box in the upper-left corner of the window and select Close to close the window.)

Now that you've safely stored the new table definition, you can exit Access if you need to take a break.

Chapter Wrap-Up

You did a lot of work in this chapter! You specified each of the fields and their data types. Some of the data types, such as the Text data types, need to have properties specified, such as their width, so that Access will not give them too much space in the database.

In one sense, you've now created a file folder for the tenant data in this sample database. You told Access exactly what kind of data will go in the file folder (tenant data) and exactly what that data should look like by specifying the fields and their properties (Tenant ID, Tenant Name, and so on).

Diving In

- After you create a table, define the fields for the table using the table definition window.

- Give each field in your table a name, data type, and description. The description is optional.

- Try to create tables that have at least one unique field. (If you do not, Access can add a unique field for you.) Customer ID numbers, product codes, and Social Security numbers make good unique field candidates for the primary key that you'll use later for searching through your table.

- After you've added a field, you can set other properties, such as the field width for Text fields.

Sunk

- Don't accept the default names Table1, Table2, and so on for your table names. Instead, make up meaningful names so that later you'll be able to find the table you want.

- Don't feel as if all records must have data for all fields. For example, many of Laura Landlady's tenants will still be living in her houses, and those tenants will have blanks for their Date Moved Out values when Laura enters data into the table created in this chapter.

8

What Are the Three Rules of Proper Computing?

Back Up, Back Up, and Back Up

- *Getting Ready to Back Up* 86
- *Making a Windows Backup* 88
- *You're Now Practicing Safe Computing!* 91

Before going any further, you must learn how to save your work. Designing a table only to find that you've accidentally erased it is not pleasant. Even worse, designing a *bunch* of tables and adding a *lot* of data and *then* accidentally erasing the database can ruin your whole day.

You are not always the culprit behind corrupted or deleted files. Power failures, power surges, people tripping over your computer's power plug, and machine breakdown can all lead to frustrated Access users.

YIKES!

It's a sickening thought, but if you use any computer long enough, the hard disk *will* go bad. Anything mechanical is subject to wear and tear, and your hard disk is no exception.

If you or someone else routinely backs up your computer's files, you are probably safe from disaster, but even if your files are routinely backed up, you should learn the skills in this chapter to back up individual database files. Before making any major changes to a database, you should back up the database so that you can go back to the original if you mess things up too much.

Getting Ready to Back Up

Most computer books mention backing up, and some of them *preach* backing up, but backing up is usually mentioned in an afterthought kind of way in the back of the book. So many people (including the author, I hate to admit) now back up not because they know it is a good thing to do, but because they lost their hard disk once when they didn't have a backup. Ever since, they've been true believers.

HMM... Backups are like fire insurance—you hope you never need either. You hope that the time you spend backing up is a total waste because if it is, and you never use the backup, then you've never had a disk problem or goofed and erased a database.

The concept of backing up disk files is simple. As Figure 8.1 shows, backing up simply means copying one or more files from the hard disk to a diskette, to a set of diskettes, or to a tape if your computer has a tape drive.

Figure 8.1.

A backup is just a copy of one or more files.

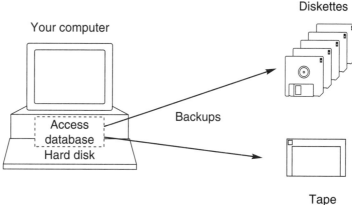

 PSST! Keep *off-site* backups. That means to keep a set of recent backup disks somewhere other than the same location as your computer. Stick the backups in your briefcase you take with you, or in your car trunk. If there was a fire around your computer and both your computer and the backups got destroyed, the backups wouldn't be worth much.

PSST! If you have a tape drive, or if you use a backup program such as PC Tools, the backup method you use might be different from the one presented here. Also, the following instructions explain how to back up individual Access database files, not entire hard disk systems.

HMM... Unlike competing database products, an Access database is easy to back up because all of its components (the data, tables, forms, and so on) reside in a single file. The name of your database is the first part of the filename, and the Access database file extension is always MDB. Therefore, the RENTALS database you have been creating is stored on the disk in a single file named RENTALS.MDB.

Making a Windows Backup

If you are not running Windows, do so now. If you are running Access, exit Access and return to the Windows desktop.

YIKES!

Be sure to close the RENTALS database (with File Close Database) before you attempt to back up the database. (This is true of any database you want to back up.) Access will not release a file for backing up until you have closed the file. If you are not running Access, you don't have to worry about closing the database.

HMM... Windows makes it easy for you to switch to another session and back up while editing your data inside Access. Be aware that an open database file cannot be backed up.

You would follow these steps to back up Laura Landlady's rental property database:

1. Insert a formatted diskette in drive A:. (If your diskette drive B: holds disks with a higher capacity than A:, change the A: in the following instructions to B:.)

2. Click with the mouse pointer over the Main program group icon if the Main window is not already open on your Windows desktop screen.

3. Double-click the File Manager icon (the filing cabinet).

4. Select the disk drive icon that contains the Access database. Figure 8.2 shows drive G: being selected.

5. Open the Access directory from the list of directories on the left side of the screen. Depending on the size of your File Manager window, you might have to click on the scroll bar to find the Access directory.

6. Drag (by clicking and holding down the mouse button) the RENTALS.MDB file from the list in the right-hand window to the drive lettered A: at the top of the window.

7. Select File Copy... from the File Manager's menu. The File Manager will have filled in the From filename for you.

Fun Fact

Nothing is more pleasing after you lose a database than restoring from a recent backup and seeing that all your work is back again. Well, maybe chocolate ice cream is more pleasing, but restoring a backup isn't fattening.

Windows will begin copying the file from the hard disk to
your diskette drive after displaying a dialog box which
verifies that you want to perform the copy operation you
just requested.

Figure 8.2.

*Selecting the
Access disk
drive icon.*

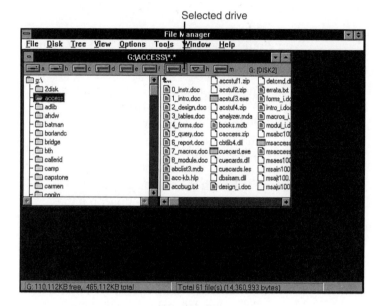

PSST!   If your diskette does not have enough free space to hold
the database file, Windows prompts you to insert another
diskette into the drive (with the dialog box shown in Figure 8.3) so that the copying can continue onto the second
disk. This process continues until the entire file is backed
up, even if several disks are needed to hold the file.

Figure 8.3.

Windows distributes the file over several diskettes if needed.

8. Select File Exit to return to the Windows desktop. You can close the Main program group (Ctrl+F4) and return to what you were doing.

You can use this same procedure for backing up any Access database. You can copy the database file to a different disk drive (different from A:) by dragging its filename to a different disk drive icon.

As an extra precaution, always back up the SYSTEM.MDA file as well. This file keeps track of your system's settings and is most important if several people share the same Access-based PC.

You're Now Practicing Safe Computing!

Now that you can back up a database file, you are ready to experiment all you want. The only way to learn a program such as Access is to use it. Before you try anything new (and possibly destructive to the database), you can back up the file and restore it anew if you need to.

PSST! Restoring a backed-up file is just a matter of reversing the drive letters (for instance, you would want Windows to copy the database file from A: to C:) in the previous instructions.

Chapter Wrap-Up

This chapter taught you how to back up your database file. To back up, you need only to activate the Windows File Manager and move your database name from the hard disk drive's listing to the name of the diskette you are backing up to.

By backing up, you tuck away your database so that you can recover from a problem that might occur.

Diving In

- Back up any database file before experimenting with something new and before making any drastic changes to your database.

- Back up your files regularly to avert a disaster in case your disk drive fails.

- Use the Windows File Manager to back up easily from the hard disk to a floppy disk.

Sunk

- Don't store your backup disks close to your computer. If there was a fire, your backups would be destroyed along with the original files. Keep off-site backups.

9

Can I Change a Table Definition?

Access Enables You to Rearrange Your Tables Easily

- Preparing to Change the Table's Structure 94
- Adding Fields 95
- Adding Fields Behind the Others 96
- Inserting New Fields Between Existing Ones 97
- Deleting Fields Is a Snap 98
- Messing with the Table 100

While creating your first table, did you think that you might not have included enough fields? What if the original order of the fields is not the best? What if you put a field in a table only to decide later that you don't need that field? After you design a table, nothing is written in stone—that's the great thing about Access. Access makes it easy to modify your table's structures any time you want, even after putting data into the table.

This chapter shows you how to change the structure of a table. While changing a table's structure, you'll see how Access takes full advantage of the Windows environment. You can adjust a table's fields by pointing, dragging, and clicking with the mouse without having to learn any commands as you would have to do with other database products on the market.

Preparing to Change the Table's Structure

Laura Landlady decides that she would like to add some notes about each tenant she rents to. You will often find yourself needing to do the same thing with your people-related fields. There are certain items about people that don't always fit a uniform field structure. For example, Laura wants to track the tenants' family members' names so that she'll be able to ask about them by name when she speaks to the tenant on the phone. Also, some tenants have special needs, such as needing to pay on the 15th day of the month rather than the first day.

When you need to keep track of arbitrary data, data that does not always fit a field structure, and data that is not uniform for every record, add a Memo field to your table.

To make any change to a table's structure, open the database that contains the table you want changed. If you see a database window on-screen already, look at the title of the database at the top of the

window to see which database is open. For this chapter's exercises, open Laura's RENTALS database if it is not already open.

 **HMM...** When you opened your very first database window, there was nothing in the white space next to the six buttons. Now there is a line next to the Table button that reads `Tenant Data`. You created this table in Chapter 7, "How Do I Describe Fields?" As you add more tables, you'll see their names listed here too.

Click the Table button of the database window, and make sure that `Tenant` is highlighted. Click Design because you want to change the design of the table. (You would use New to create an additional table from scratch and Open to add data to an existing table, as you'll do in the next section of the book.)

Access displays the familiar table definition with all the fields listed that you added in the preceding chapter.

Adding Fields

There are two ways to add fields to an existing table depending on whether you want to add the new fields at the end of the table or between two other fields. We'll add two fields using each method.

PSST! The order in which you list fields in a table structure has little bearing on the table's use. You can report a table's data in any field order that you want regardless of the order of the fields listed in the structure. Nevertheless, the fields are listed in the order in which you structured them if you don't override the order when you report the data. Therefore, try to order the fields loosely based on the order in which you would prefer to see them.

Adding Fields Behind the Others

The first field to add is the Memo field described earlier. Adding a field to the end of the table is easy. Using the keyboard or clicking with the mouse, move the cursor to the box under the Field Name column.

PSST!   A quick way to see which line your cursor is on is to look at the thin gray column of blocks to the left of the Field Name column. The black arrow (called the *row selector*) points to whatever field is *active,* meaning the field you can modify or add to.

Type Notes as the field name, select Memo from the Data Type column (by clicking the downward-pointing arrow or pressing Shift+down arrow), and type the following description: Misc. notes about the tenant and family

Skip This, It's Technical

A Memo field can be long. Really long. Up to 32,000 characters long! The field properties for Memo (in the lower pane) don't include a Field Size property as text fields do. Use Memo fields whenever you need them, but don't use them for field data that you would want to search on (such as an address) because searching Memo fields is very inefficient.

Inserting New Fields Between Existing Ones

Suppose that Laura Landlady wants to keep track of the name of her tenant's employer in addition to the work phone number. She would need to add a Text field to the table. The natural location for the name of the employer would be right before the employer's phone number in the table.

Use the Edit pull-down menu to add new fields to the table. Follow these steps to insert the new Text field in the table:

1. Click the mouse (or move the highlight with the keyboard) over the row containing the Phone Number (work) field. When you insert a new field, Access always inserts the new field above the currently highlighted field. Therefore, you are now inserting a new field before the Phone Number (work) field.

2. Select Edit Insert Row. Access opens up a space for the new field, as Figure 9.1 shows.

Figure 9.1.

Making room to insert a new field.

Field Name	Data Type	Description
Tenant ID	Text	Uniquely identifies each tenant
Tenant's Name	Text	Last, then first separated by commas
Property ID	Text	ID of this tenant's property
Phone Number (home)	Text	Tenant's home phone number
Phone Number (work)	Text	Tenant's work phone number
Date Moved In	Date/Time	Date moved into property
Date Moved Out	Date/Time	Date moved out of property
Rent Amount	Currency	Monthly rent
Deposit Amount	Currency	Security deposit
Pet Deposit?	Yes/No	Is there a pet?

Table: Tenant Data

Field Properties

A field name can be up to 64 characters long, including spaces. Press F1 for help on field names.

3.   Enter the new field as follows: Type `Employer` for the field name, `Text` as the Data Type, and `The tenant's employer` as the Description.

4.   Limit the size of the new field by clicking the Field Size box (in the lower pane of the window) and entering `25`.

That's it. You've added a new field. If there had been data in the table (which there is not at this point, but we'll enter some soon), you still could have added the field just as easily.

YIKES!

If you add a new field to a table that contains data, the records that are already in the file will contain blanks in the newly added field until you replace the blanks with data.

Deleting Fields Is a Snap

Deleting a field in a table is even easier than inserting one. We won't walk through an example here because deleting a field is so easy when you know how to insert one.

To delete a field, click anywhere within the row of the field you want to delete, and select Edit Delete Row. If data is in the table (there is none in the RENTALS database yet), Access displays the warning shown in Figure 9.2 just to give you a chance to change your mind.

PSST!   If you delete a field by mistake, select Edit Undo (Ctrl+Z). Access returns the deleted field to its original position.

Figure 9.2.

The warning box you'll see if you delete a field from a table with data.

For practice, insert an Employer's Address field and then delete it. Access follows your wishes without complaints.

YIKES!

If you are going to make several changes to a table, especially the deletion of one or more fields, save the database first with File Save. If you change too much, you can always retrieve the original table intact up until the time you save it again under the same name.

Skip This, It's Technical

Well, even though it's technical, maybe you should pay attention. After you add data to a table, you need to be careful about deleting fields and changing field properties such as names and sizes. Many times, these types of changes will have little effect on your existing data, but the deletion or change could negatively affect the data in the table. If you find that you need to change a table's structure after adding data to the table, Access enables you to. Back up your database first (under a new name so that you can recover it if you need to) just in case your change affects the table's data negatively. Your *User's Guide* that came with Access describes the caveats of modifying a table's structure after data is entered, but the bottom line is this: make the structure's changes *one* at a time. In other words, if you want to change the name of a field and change its field size, change the name first, save the table, and then change the field size.

Messing with the Table

Access provides two additional table tools that you will almost certainly find useful. With the mouse, you can change the height of each row in the table window and rearrange any of the rows. These capabilities are extremely Windows-like and demonstrate the real power of a graphical user environment such as Windows.

Depending on your graphics adapter and monitor, the table structure might be hard to read with a lot of rows showing at once. You can easily change the height of the field structure's lines (but not the size of the font) by following these steps:

1. Move the mouse cursor to the thin gray column at the left of the Field Name column (the column where the black row-selector arrow resides).

2. Slowly move the mouse cursor down the column until it changes to the *row resizing* shape with an arrow pointing both up and down.

3. Drag (hold down the mouse button while moving) the mouse down a little (a few fractions of an inch). As you drag the mouse, the dividing line between the rows will move with the row resizing pointer.

4. Let up on the mouse after you've dragged the mouse a little way. Access resizes all rows to the new height. The more you resize, the more space there is between the rows, but the fewer rows you can see at once.

YIKES!

Be careful. Making the rows too large wastes screen real
estate that could be used for more of the table structure, as
shown in Figure 9.3. Also, resizing the rows too small makes the
labels within the rows difficult or impossible to read.

Figure 9.3.

*After an over-
zealous field
height resizing.*

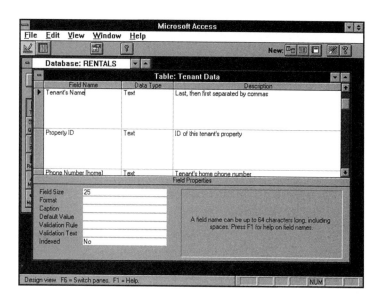

In a similar manner, you can resize the width of the three columns
on the table structure screen. Laura Landlady feels that too much
width is being given to the Field Name field. The longest field
name is Phone Number (home), so the column has to be only
wide enough to display this field name. Squeezing the Field
Name column will give more room to the Description column
in case Laura wants to add a longer description later.

To resize a column's width, move the mouse cursor over the gray line atop the table structure window right below the title bar. The cursor should be resting somewhere over the line that labels the Field Name, Data Type, and Description columns. Slowly position the mouse cursor between the Field Name title and the Data Type title, and you'll see the cursor change to the column resizing cursor.

Drag the cursor (which drags the dividing line between the columns) to the left until the dividing line leaves just enough room for the Phone Number (home) field, and let up on the mouse. Access adds the extra room to the Description field for longer descriptions.

Another snazzy Windows-like feature is the rearranging capability of Access. Suppose that Laura Landlady decided that she wanted the Employer field to appear after the Phone Number (work) field. Rearranging these fields requires only clicking and moving the mouse as described here:

1. Move the mouse cursor to the thin gray column to the left of the Field Name column.

2. Click the gray box next to the Employer field. After you let up on the mouse button, Access highlights the entire row.

3. Click and drag the mouse pointer slowly down one row. You'll notice that the mouse cursor changes shape a bit by outlining a box below the cursor. The box indicates that you are moving something (carrying something in a box). As you slowly move down to the next row, you'll see a dark line appear between the Phone Number (work) field and the Date Moved In field. It is this dark line between these two rows that you are looking for.

4. Let up on the mouse button, and Access moves the Employer field so that it rests below the Phone Number (work) field.

HMM... You could have first deleted the Employer field, then inserted it in the new location, but that would have taken much more work. After you get used to rearranging with the mouse, you'll be glad that Access is Windows-based!

Chapter Wrap-Up

In this chapter, you learned all the ways to rearrange and resize your table's format. You are still working on honing the table's definition. The first time you create a table, you'll find that you'll want to make adjustments to its field order and sizes.

Using the menus, you can add and delete fields as shown in this chapter. Using just the mouse, you can resize and rearrange fields so that they appear just the way you want them to. Of course, the look and arrangement of the data itself is of most importance to a database, but getting the table's definition right is important also so that the data has a good structure in which to reside.

Diving In

- Feel free to change your table's structure. Access makes changing the structure easy.

- Add new fields at the end of the table of fields by clicking with the mouse and entering the new field's information.

- Add new fields between other fields with the Edit Insert Row menu.

- Delete fields with the Edit Delete Row menu.

- Resize row sizes and column widths—it's as easy as clicking the mouse and dragging to the new sizes.

Sunk

- If your table has data, don't get carried away with making all the changes at once. Back up the database before you begin, and then make the table changes one at a time while saving between each one. This helps ensure a smooth table change with the least impact on your existing data.

- Don't delete and insert fields if you want to rearrange your table's field order. Learn the rearranging mouse skills described at the end of this chapter.

Part III
Working with the Data

How Do I Put Data in a Table?

Use the Datasheet View

- Getting Ready to Enter Data 108
- The Datasheet View 110
- Let's Enter Some Data 111
- Special Data Considerations 114
- Managing the Datasheet 115

If you've ever entered data in a spreadsheet, you'll think that entering data in an Access database is easy. You can enter and edit data in a table using a *datasheet view*. A datasheet view is nothing more than a spreadsheet-like row and column table on your screen in which you can enter data. If you've never used a spreadsheet program, that's OK too. After learning about Access datasheet views, you'll have a leg up on learning spreadsheets!

This chapter teaches you how to enter data using the Laura Landlady's Tenant Data table as an example. After you master this chapter's concepts, you'll be able to add and edit data in any table that you create.

PSST!   To *edit* data means to change it in some way. When you edit data in a table, you are changing some data in one or more records.

Getting Ready to Enter Data

After defining a table's structure, you can then enter real data into that structure. In a way, a table's structure is like a blank form. If you were applying for entrance into a certain college, you would fill out a form that the college gives you. The form itself contains nothing but blank fields. After you fill out the form, the form contains what is known as *live* data.

Before colleges computerized their records, they would give enrolling students blank forms, the students would fill out the forms, and the college would file the forms in a large filing cabinet. The student's data could change. A student might move or get married. When a student's data changed, a clerk would open the filing cabinet drawer, pull out the student's form, and write in the change.

Today, colleges are computerized, but even so, the process of record keeping is exactly the same. Instead of keeping the paper forms,

however, the college keeps database records. Now when a student enrolls, the clerk sits in front of a computer and enters the student's data directly into the computer. If a student's data changes, the clerk displays the student's information on-screen and changes it then and there.

YIKES!

Have we just jumped from an easy system (the paper system) to a difficult system (the computer) without any gains? Of course not. The computer can find student records much more quickly than a person manually looking through a filing cabinet. There is a lot more that the computer can do with the data too. With computers networked all over the campus, *anybody* with the right access (now where have we heard *that* word...) can bring up the student's data and look at it or change it depending on the need.

There are two primary ways to enter data into an Access database; this part of the book explains both of them. They are

- A datasheet view

- A form

This chapter's introduction explained that a datasheet view is nothing more than a spreadsheet-like grid of your table's data. This chapter shows you all about the datasheet view and how to use it. Starting in Chapter 12, "What Is a Form?" you'll learn how to create a form on-screen that looks just like a paper form, but the Access form will be easier to change if you make mistakkkkes!

PSST! A datasheet view enables you to enter, view, and edit several records at once, whereas a form view enables you to enter, view, or edit only a single record at a time.

The Datasheet View

Return to the RENTALS database window. If you just started Access, open the database with the File Open Database... menu item. At the database window, click the Tables button to display the Tenant table if it is not already displayed.

The Tenant table is highlighted (displayed in reverse lettering) because it is the only table in the database at this time. Instead of pressing the Design button as you've done before to work on the table's structure, click the Open button. When you do, you'll see the screen shown in Figure 10.1. The Tenant table is shown in its datasheet view.

Figure 10.1.

Getting ready to enter data in the datasheet view.

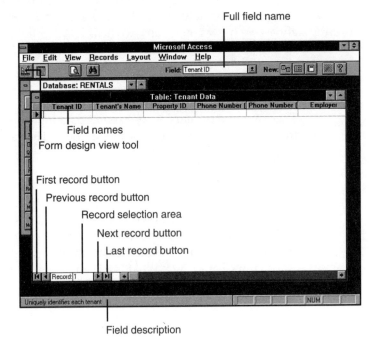

Full field name

Field names

Form design view tool

First record button

Previous record button

Record selection area

Next record button

Last record button

Field description

YIKES!

If you've used a spreadsheet, you might not think that this datasheet view looks much like a spreadsheet. There are no records in the table yet. After you enter some data, the familiar (to some readers) spreadsheet-like row and column grid appearance will begin to emerge. Unlike with a blank spreadsheet, Access does not display lots of blank rows and columns if there is no data in the table.

In the datasheet, the rows represent records in the table and the columns are the fields. As you type data into the datasheet, you are typing data directly into the table. Across the top of the datasheet are the field names that you assigned when you defined the table's structure. By using descriptive field names, you made the datasheet view easier to use.

YIKES!

You cannot see all the Tenant table's fields. All the fields are there, and if you want to see them, you can press Tab or the right arrow to move the cursor to the left until the extreme-right fields come into view. You can also use the mouse to click the horizontal scroll bar at the bottom of the window to see the extreme-right fields.

Let's Enter Some Data

Entering data into a table using the datasheet view is easy and intuitive. Move the cursor to the first field (Tenant ID), and enter a value. For the first Tenant ID, type WAL1. Press Enter or Tab, and the cursor moves to the start of the next field.

Laura is using the first three letters of the tenant's last name plus a number for the tenant's ID. If Laura had two tenants (in different houses) named Wallace, the second tenant's ID would be WAL2.

YIKES!

When you typed the w in WAL1, a new record opened up and a pencil icon appeared next to the first row. The pencil is letting you know that you are typing data into a record (as if you didn't know!). The pencil will go away as soon as you move to the next opened-up record by pressing the down arrow (don't press the down arrow right now).

PSST! As always, you can use the Insert and Delete keys to insert and delete mistakes in Access text boxes.

Finish the first record by typing the following data:

Field Name	Data
Tenant's Name	Wallace, Dale
Property ID	H1
Phone Number (home)	(918) 627-2033
Phone Number (work)	(918) 838-9233
Employer	Williams, Inc.
Date Moved In	5/1/93
Date Moved Out	(leave blank)
Rent Amount	410.00
Deposit Amount	125.00
Pet Deposit?	No
Notes	Spouse: Lisa

PSST! You cannot see the entire field name at the top of every column. Some field names, such as Phone Number (home), will not fit in the datasheet view's column width space. When you are entering data in these fields, Access displays the full field name on the toolbar. Move the cursor to a long field name and see how the full name displays on the toolbar even though the name is too long to fit at the top of the column.

HMM... As you enter data, at the bottom of the screen Access displays the field's description that you gave when you added each field to the table's structure.

After you enter all the data, your table will look like the one in Figure 10.2. Access placed the cursor in the Tenant ID field of the next row. You might be wondering how Laura Landlady determines the Property ID. Laura has houses, duplexes, and small apartment buildings (she is just wallowing in rental income!), so her Property ID field indicates the type of building with an *H*, a *D*, or an *A*. We'll learn about her properties when we add a property table later in the book.

Figure 10.2.

After entering the first record's data.

Row selector

Tenant ID	Tenant's Name	Property ID	Phone Number (	Phone Number (	Employer
WAL1	Wallace, Dale	H1	(918) 627-2033	(918) 838-9233	Williams, Inc.

Table: Tenant Data

YIKES!

If you make a mistake after entering the row, don't worry, because the mistake is easy to correct. Click the mouse cursor over the mistake, and the text cursor appears for your corrections.

Special Data Considerations

Access is very forgiving when you enter specially formatted data such as dates, times, money amounts, and Memo field values. The way you enter data in these fields is basically any way that feels best to you! For example, you can enter a date in Date fields with any of the following formats:

```
5/1/93
05/01/93
5/1/1993
May 1, 1993
May 1 1993
```

YIKES!

The format you use to enter a date isn't necessarily the way the date ends up looking. After you enter a date and move to the next field, Access formats the appearance of the date in a predefined manner as described in the field's properties. By default, Access displays dates in the *mm/dd/yy* format.

Time can be entered in *hh:mm:ss* format, in which *hh* represents the hour, *mm* represents minutes, and *ss* represents seconds. You can either add *AM* or *PM* or use a 24-hour clock time.

PSST! If you press Ctrl+semicolon, Access automatically enters the current date. Ctrl+colon causes Access to insert the current time.

Fun Facts
Welcome to the 20th century! You are filling out one of those blank computerized forms we discussed earlier. In a couple of chapters, you'll see how to make the screen really look like a form.

The Currency fields are just as abundant with their data-entry freedoms as the Date/Time fields are. You can type a dollar sign, type the decimals, and even insert commas in numbers as you enter Currency data. After you enter a valid amount, Access redisplays the field according to the field's property.

If you enter a format that Access does not recognize, such as placing two decimal points in a dollar amount, Access displays a warning dialog box (Figure 10.3) and requires that you enter an appropriate value before moving on to the next field.

Figure 10.3.
Oops! Access lets you know if you enter a bad format.

Managing the Datasheet

Rarely is anything written in stone with Access, even the datasheet view. If you want to resize or rearrange the datasheet fields, you can do so just as you resized and rearranged the columns in the table definition window in the preceding chapter. If you shrink the width of some columns, you'll be able to see more columns at one time on the same screen.

To resize a field, move the mouse cursor over the field name at the top of the datasheet window. Position the mouse cursor on either side of the field name so that the mouse cursor becomes a resizing cursor. Click and drag the vertical bar beneath the field name left or right to shrink or increase the width of the field.

The Property ID field's data is only three characters long, so you don't need the extra space there. Shrink that column. Should you increase the size of the two phone number columns so that you can see the entire field name? Probably not, because the phone numbers themselves have plenty of room to display, and seeing the data is more important than seeing the full field name. The Pet Deposit? field can be shrunk a little, and you can also double-click the window's title bar to increase the datasheet to full-screen size.

You can drag and drop the fields on the datasheet view to rearrange the columns if you like. Follow the same steps to rearrange fields as you did when you learned to rearrange columns in the table definition window in the preceding chapter. Click twice on the field you want to move, and on the second click, drag the field to where you want to place it before letting go of the mouse button.

 **HMM...** The arrangement of your datasheet view's fields does not change the underlying table's structure.

 **PSST!** If you like, you can quickly move between the table's definition window (called the *design view*) and the datasheet view without returning first to the database window control center. The two tools at the top-left of the toolbar (shown in

Figure 10.4) are the design view tool and the datasheet view tool. Click one and then the other to move back and forth between the table's two views. As you enter data into the table, you might have a question about the underlying table structure, which is now only a click away.

Figure 10.4.

Tools for switch-ing between design view and datasheet view.

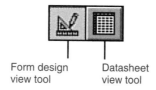

Form design   Datasheet
view tool   view tool

The next chapter shows you how to work with several records in the datasheet view. If you want to save the record you added here, select File Save. After saving, you can exit Access and take a break.

Chapter Wrap-Up

Your table now has data! This chapter explained how to use the datasheet view to add and change data in your table's structure. You have now created a database, created a table, and put one record in that table.

Rearranging and resizing a datasheet view requires no skills that you don't already possess. Use the same drag and drop techniques to size and arrange the datasheet as you did with the table's struc-ture itself in the preceding chapter. The Tenant table has only one record now, but after the next chapter, lots of data will be in the table.

Diving In

- Use the datasheet view to enter data into tables.

- Watch the screen as you enter data. Access displays the full field name at the top of the datasheet view and the field's description at the bottom of the datasheet view as you enter data.

- Enter dates, times, and currencies in whatever format makes the most sense to you. Access is generous and will let you know if you type in a format that cannot be understood.

- Quickly switch back and forth between the design view (your table's structure) and the datasheet view (your table's data) by clicking the appropriate tools.

- Resize and rearrange the datasheet fields in any order you like.

Sunk

- Don't expect to see all of your table's fields at once in the datasheet view. Scroll back and forth to display the ones you need.

Can I Manage Several Records?

Enter and Look Through the Datasheet View

- Getting More Data In 120
- Moving Around 127
- Getting a Bird's-Eye View 129
- Deleting Records 130

This chapter extends the preceding chapter's discussion about the datasheet view. After entering a few more records, you'll learn how to manage those records by searching for them and rearranging their order. You'll also jump back once to the design view and change the appearance of one of the date field's properties.

Working with several records is a breeze with the tools Access provides. You can even mess up something, such as deleting the wrong record, and Access fixes your mistake when you issue the Undo command.

Getting More Data In

Before going much further, you've got to get more data into Laura Landlady's database. There isn't much more you can learn with only a one-record table. Therefore, take a few moments to enter the records listed in Table 11.1. As you enter them, keep the following points in mind:

- The lower-left corner of the datasheet window tells you the number of the record you are entering or editing.

- Press the up arrow and down arrow to move up and down through the records if you want to correct a mistake you made in an earlier record. Ctrl+Home moves the cursor to the very first field, and Ctrl+End moves it to the very last field. The Page Up and Page Down keys scroll a window of several records up and down.

- Home moves the cursor to the first field in the current record, and End moves the cursor to the last field in the current record.

- If you are entering data into a field, such as the Memo field named Notes, keep typing. When you get to the edge of the field's data-entry box, Access shifts the text you've typed to the left to make room for more data.

● The default value for the Currency fields (such as Deposit
  Amount) is $0.00, and the default value for the Pet Deposit?
  field is No. You can change an individual field's default
  value by adding a new default value in the field's property
  pane from the design view of the table.

Here is the new data that you should enter into Laura Landlady's
Tenant table:

Table 11.1. **Laura Landlady's Tenant table.**

Field Name	Data
Record 2	
Tenant ID	JOH1
Tenant's Name	Johnson, Terrie
Property ID	H2
Phone Number (home)	(918) 123-6422
Phone Number (work)	(918) 211-7886
Employer	Jenks Public Schools
Date Moved In	11/2/92
Date Moved Out	5/30/93
Rent Amount	475.00
Deposit Amount	250.00
Pet Deposit?	Yes
Notes	Dog's name: Luke
Record 3	
Tenant ID	LAR1
Tenant's Name	Larson, Michael

continues

Table 11.1. continued

Field Name	Data
Record 3	
Property ID	A1a
Phone Number (home)	(leave blank)
Phone Number (work)	(918) 655-7522
Employer	Reed's Ramblers
Date Moved In	4/1/93
Date Moved Out	(leave blank)
Rent Amount	375.00
Deposit Amount	150.00
Pet Deposit?	Yes
Notes	Spouse: Betty, Cat: Sam
Record 4	
Tenant ID	PHI1
Tenant's Name	Philips, Mary
Property ID	H2
Phone Number (home)	(918) 870-3323
Phone Number (work)	(918) 659-8000
Employer	MPI and Company
Date Moved In	6/15/93
Date Moved Out	(leave blank)
Rent Amount	275.00
Deposit Amount	130.00

Field Name	Data

Record 4

Pet Deposit?	No
Notes	Spouse: Tim, Boy: Robert (5 yrs)

Record 5

Tenant ID	MAJ1
Tenant's Name	Majors, Heath
Property ID	A1b
Phone Number (home)	(918) 661-7521
Phone Number (work)	(405) 777-0011
Employer	Glider Properties
Date Moved In	8/12/90
Date Moved Out	(leave blank)
Rent Amount	250.00
Deposit Amount	100.00
Pet Deposit?	Yes
Notes	Spouse: Audrey, Dog: Nick

Record 6

Tenant ID	BUS1
Tenant's Name	Bush, Dan
Property ID	A1c
Phone Number (home)	(918) 949-9233
Phone Number (work)	(918) 491-5653

continues

Table 11.1. continued

Field Name	Data
Record 6	
Employer	Computer Sales
Date Moved In	6/30/93
Date Moved Out	(leave blank)
Rent Amount	300.00
Deposit Amount	125.00
Pet Deposit?	No
Notes	Spouse: Jane
Record 7	
Tenant ID	SMI1
Tenant's Name	Smith, Martha
Property ID	D1
Phone Number (home)	(918) 627-4922
Phone Number (work)	(918) 759-1234
Employer	World Travel
Date Moved In	6/1/93
Date Moved Out	(leave blank)
Rent Amount	300.00
Deposit Amount	150.00
Pet Deposit?	No
Notes	Spouse: Ollie

Field Name	Data

Record 8

Tenant ID	HIL1
Tenant's Name	Hill, Paul
Property ID	D2
Phone Number (home)	(918) 211-3905
Phone Number (work)	(918) 544-6567
Employer	Tim's Trucking
Date Moved In	3/31/93
Date Moved Out	(leave blank)
Rent Amount	400.00
Deposit Amount	250.00
Pet Deposit?	No
Notes	Spouse: Sandy

Record 9

Tenant ID	SMI2
Tenant's Name	Smith, Bill
Property ID	A1d
Phone Number (home)	(918) 444-6167
Phone Number (work)	(918) 409-7423
Employer	City Courthouse
Date Moved In	10/1/92
Date Moved Out	(leave blank)
Rent Amount	230.00

continues

Table 11.1. continued

Field Name	Data
Record 9	
Deposit Amount	100.00
Pet Deposit?	No
Notes	Spouse: Abby
Record 10	
Tenant ID	ADA1
Tenant's Name	Adams, Carly
Property ID	H3
Phone Number (home)	(918) 863-2910
Phone Number (work)	(918) 466-0055
Employer	Widgets, Ltd.
Date Moved In	11/2/93
Date Moved Out	(leave blank)
Rent Amount	300.00
Deposit Amount	175.00
Pet Deposit?	Yes
Notes	Spouse: Kent, Dog: Rover, Daughter: Julie

YIKES!

Take the time to enter all this data. The practice is worth the effort, and we'll use this data. When you finish, your screen will look like the one in Figure 11.1.

Figure 11.1.

*After entering
lots of records.*

Print preview tool

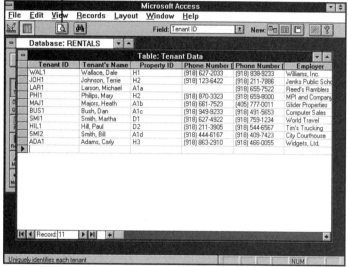

Skip This, It's Technical

If you are entering a field that has the same value as the
preceding record's corresponding field, press Ctrl+apostrophe.
Access copies the preceding record's data into the current field. If
you were entering addresses for local residents, for example, the
city and state fields would make excellent candidates for the
Ctrl+apostrophe ditto copy of data.

Moving Around

With only 10 records of data, you won't need to move around in
the table much, but doing so will give you practice that you'll need
when you have thousands of records to move through. Being able

to get around and find data is vital to maintaining a powerful and usable database system.

PSST! The fastest way to move to a specific record is to press F5. The cursor moves down to the lower-left corner box that holds the current record number. Type a new record number, and Access moves the cursor to the first field in that record.

You can click the first record, previous record, next record, and last record buttons that surround the record number at the bottom of the screen to move forward and backward through the datasheet.

HMM... Just for grins, jump to the design view by pressing the design view tool. Now, return to the datasheet view, and you'll see something new. Access has alphabetized the records by Tenant ID! The automatic datasheet sort is performed on the table's primary key field.

There is never a need to insert a record between two others. Every time you load the datasheet, Access sorts the records by primary key order.

YIKES!

Don't worry if you need to see data in a different order from the order in which you entered the data. There are plenty of ways to sort records in any order you want, as you'll find out later.

Getting a Bird's-Eye View

If you have used a word processor before, you might be familiar with a feature called *print preview*. In a word processor, you can use print preview to view (on-screen) a report as it will appear on paper if you print the report. Viewing the report on the screen is faster than printing, and it doesn't waste paper.

You can preview the datasheet by selecting File Print Preview from the menu. Instead of selecting from the menu, however, you can use the magnifying-glass-over-paper tool on the toolbar to select File Print Preview for you. Click the magnifying-glass-over-paper tool now. You'll see something like the screen in Figure 11.2.

Fun Fact
The print preview is Access's WYSIWYG feature described in Chapter 1, "What's Access All About?" WYSIWYG is even more fun to say than to use.

Figure 11.2.
Getting a glimpse of the entire datasheet.

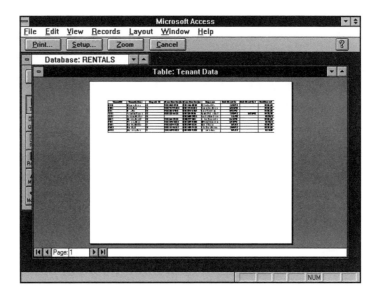

YIKES!

What's the matter, you can't read the text? The purpose of print preview is not to read individual lines but to see what your datasheet would look like if you printed it to paper by selecting File Print....

PSST!

You can zoom in and get a closer look by moving the mouse cursor over the area you want to read. Notice that the cursor changes to a magnifying glass, indicating that you can take a closer look. Press the mouse button, and you can read the text underneath the cursor. Press Esc to return to the datasheet view (you cannot edit while looking at the print preview).

Deleting Records

If you want to, you can delete records in the datasheet. To delete a single record, click the thin gray box next to the record you want to delete (this is the row selector's column). Press Delete (you can also choose Edit Delete from the menu), and Access deletes the record. Access gives you one chance, however, to get the record back by displaying a dialog box warning (shown in Figure 11.3).

To delete a range of records, select the first record in the range, and then click the last record in the range *while holding down the Shift key*. Access highlights the range of records. Press Delete to delete all the records.

Figure 11.3.

Giving you a chance to change your mind.

PSST! Ctrl+hyphen also deletes the record you've selected.

YIKES!

Don't delete any records at this time. You spent too much effort typing all this practice data to lose it now!

Chapter Wrap-Up

This chapter walked you through the steps needed to add several records to Laura Landlady's growing database of tenants. After you've entered several records, you can move through the records by using the keyboard's direction keys (such as down arrow and Page Up). You can also press F5 to jump to a specific record.

You will need to insert and delete records in your tables as time goes by. Insert all new records at the end of the table because Access rearranges the records in the primary key field's order anyway. You can delete single records or a range of records by highlighting the record or records to delete and pressing Delete.

Diving In

- Practice entering several records so that you'll know how to maneuver around and within them.

- When you have lots of records, you can use the F5 key to move quickly to any record.

- Use print preview to look at a bird's-eye view of your datasheet.

Sunk

- Don't try to insert a record between two others in the datasheet. There is no need to insert records between two existing ones. Access sorts the records by the primary key field every time you load the datasheet.

What Is a Form?

A Form Is Another View of Table Data

- Get Ready to Be Amazed! 135
- Moving Around with Forms 139
- Changing Data 140
- Adding Data 141
- Deleting Records in Form View 142
- Save Your Work! 142

Although a datasheet view is easy to use, and although a datasheet view is especially useful to those who have used a spreadsheet before, the purpose of the computer is to help people in any way it can. When computerizing your records, you want to make it as easy as possible for the person at the keyboard to use the program that is running.

Often, a database program such as Access reduces the amount of paperwork needed. For example, a credit agency might use Access to keep track of loan applications that the borrowers fill out. As borrowers bring in their completed applications, a clerk types the data from the application into an Access table. Although a datasheet works fine, a form works even better!

Doesn't it make sense to duplicate on-screen the appearance of the paper form that contains the source data? The closer in appearance that the Access database is to the paper form, the more easily and quickly the clerk can transfer the data from the application to the database.

This chapter introduces you to two topics: form design and AccessWizards. We'll use the helpful on-line *FormWizard,* a part of AccessWizards that you read about in Chapter 4, "How Can I Get Help?" to create an on-screen form for Laura Landlady's tenants.

PSST! Forms are just another way of doing what you do with datasheets. Using a form, you can enter, look at, and change data in a table. The advantage of an Access form is that it looks like a paper form and is a familiar interface for end users. The disadvantage of forms is that you can look at only a single record at a time.

Get Ready to Be Amazed!

You're going to be surprised at the amount of built-in power Access provides when you want to create a new form. Using the step-by-step help that FormWizard provides, you'll be creating a form just by answering a few simple questions.

HMM... After you practice creating the form described in this chapter, you'll be able to generate your own forms for your own applications. FormWizard creates forms by asking you questions. If you design a form using FormWizard and don't know the answer to one of FormWizard's questions, press Enter and accept the default answer. Most of the time, the default answer is the right one.

YIKES! Why are you designing a form? For the same reason you design a table before storing data in the table. You must tell Access exactly what your form is to look like. Luckily, FormWizard makes this task easy.

To develop a form for Laura Landlady's Tenant table, open the database if it is not already open, and click the Form button in the database window. Follow these steps to create a form using FormWizard:

1.   Select New. Access displays a New Form window. From this window you can use FormWizard to help you create the form, or create one from scratch.

2. Click the arrow on the Select A Table/Query box, and select the Tenant Data table.

3. Because FormWizard provides you with a near-perfect form every time, without the hassles involved in creating a form from scratch, click the FormWizards button. Access displays the form selection screen shown in Figure 12.1.

Figure 12.1.
Getting ready to choose a form design.

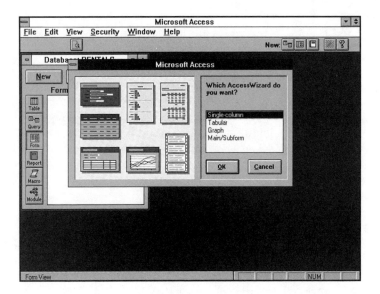

 HMM... Unlike designing a table or datasheet, designing a form is simply a matter of selecting from the different form designs inside FormWizard.

4. Select Single-column and click the OK button. After a brief pause, Access displays the field selection screen. FormWizard is asking exactly what fields you want displayed on the form and what fields in the table you don't

want displayed. Laura wants all the tenants' fields displayed, so select the >> button to move all the Available fields to the Field order on form list.

PSST!   If you wanted only a few of the table's fields to end up on the form, you would highlight a field in the Available fields list one at a time, clicking the > button to move the selected field to the Field order on form list.

5. Select Next> to move to the next screen in FormWizard. You'll see the form-style selection screen shown in Figure 12.2.

Figure 12.2.
Choosing a style for your form.

Sample look appears here

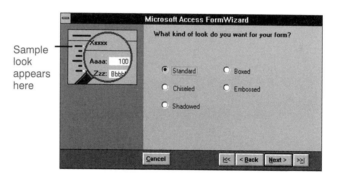

 Any time during your use of FormWizard, you can return to a previous screen and change a selection by choosing <Back.

6. There are several form appearances, from Standard to Embossed. Click each of the buttons to see what the resulting form will look like (the magnifying glass shows the result). Select Embossed and then choose Next>.

7. Access wants to know what title you prefer at the top of the form when the form is displayed for the end user. Rather than Tenant Data (the default title is always the name of the table), type My Tenants for the new form's title, and click Open to display the form. Access displays a full-featured data-entry form right before your eyes.

Maximize the form's window so that you see all the fields. Access has displayed the table's first record, the record with the Tenant ID ADA1, as shown in Figure 12.3.

Figure 12.3.

Your form is already designed!

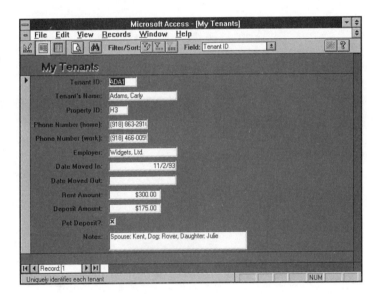

YIKES!

There is a slight problem with the form. Look at the phone-number fields. The fields are not wide enough to hold the phone-number data. You'll learn how to widen these fields in Chapter 15, "How Do I Improve My Form's Appearance?" Access is a good guesser when it comes to designing your forms, but there's always room for improvement.

Moving Around with Forms

The form looks just like a paper form might look. If Laura Landlady gives her new tenants a blank form to fill out that contains the same fields as this computerized form, and in the same order, Laura can very easily transfer that information into this form. Although forms show only a single record at a time (unlike datasheet views), a form is a much better tool for looking at an individual record.

  On a datasheet, you can see lots of records but not *all* of each record, because the right side of the screen chops off the rightmost records. In a form view, you can see all of a record's fields on one screen.

There are several ways to move through the records in the form view. The up arrow, down arrow, Tab, and Shift+Tab move the cursor from one field to another. The Page Up and Page Down keys move to the next and preceding record in the table. The record number in the bottom of the screen displays the location of the current record in the table.

There is a record scroll bar at the bottom of the screen that you also can use to move from record to record. Clicking the left and right arrows causes the preceding or next record to appear. Clicking the outside arrows makes the form display the first or last record in the table.

  If you want to jump to a record quickly and you know the record number, press F5 and type the record number you want to see. Access displays that record in the form view.

Another neat feature of the form view is that Access enables you to move to a datasheet view from the form view quickly. Figure 12.4

shows the toolbar at the top of the form. Click the datasheet tool, and Access displays the table in datasheet view. Click the form tool to see the form again.

Figure 12.4.

Using the toolbar, you can change views quickly.

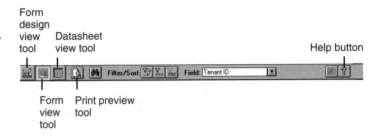

Form design view tool

Datasheet view tool

Help button

Form view tool

Print preview tool

PSST! You can click the form design tool if you like, but don't change anything if you do. The form design view is the view that enables you to change and rearrange the form, as you'll see in Chapter 15, "How Do I Improve My Form's Appearance?"

Changing Data

If you display a record in a form and want to change any of the data on the form, move the cursor to that field, press F2 to enter the field-editing mode (or click with the mouse), and type a new value. A pencil appears in the left column indicating that data has been changed, but the change has not yet been written to the disk. When you move to a new record, Access saves the change to the table.

YIKES!

If you make a change to a field and decide you don't want that change saved after all, select Edit Undo Current, and Access puts the data back the way it was before you made changes.

Adding Data

When you write Access applications that a non-Access person will use, you will most likely create data-entry forms so that the user can add data in a familiar paper form format. There are two ways to add data to a table while in form view. One method is to display the last record in the table and click the next record arrow. In the Tenant table, the last record in the table is record number 10. Clicking the next record button displays a blank record's number 11.

After moving to the blank record, add the following data:

Field Name	Data
Tenant ID	DRE1
Tenant's Name	Drew, Kim
Property ID	H4
Phone Number (home)	(918) 776-4321
Phone Number (work)	(918) 778-5330
Employer	Oklahoma Oil
Date Moved In	5/30/93
Date Moved Out	
Rent Amount	450.00
Deposit Amount	225.00
Pet Deposit?	Yes
Notes	Spouse: Chris, Cat: Purfect

A data-entry form's Yes/No data type field (the Pet Deposit? field in the Tenant Data table) can be checked with an × with a mouse click or a press of the Spacebar.

When you finish entering data for the last field, Access displays a new blank record.

You can add data to the form in another way too. Select Records Data Entry, and Access displays a blank form. Access hides all the other records in the table so that you can see only the newly added records as you enter them. If you want to see all the records again, select Records Show All Records, and Access returns all the records to the form view.

Deleting Records in Form View

To delete a record, click the thin gray vertical selection bar at the left of the form's fields. Press the Delete key, and after Access verifies that you really want to delete the record, the record is erased.

Save Your Work!

Access has not saved your form design yet (just the data you changed or entered). When you save your form, Access enables you to give the form a name so that you can retrieve it later. To save the form, follow these steps:

1. Select File Close.

2. Access warns you that you haven't saved your form. Answer Yes to the dialog box to indicate that you do indeed want to save the form (you went to too much trouble not to save your work!).

3. Instead of using Access's generous name `form1`, type the easy-to-remember form name `Tenant Form` in the Save As dialog box. Access returns to the database window, where you can then do something else with the database or exit Access.

Chapter Wrap-Up

After mastering this chapter, you can now create complex forms just by answering a few questions from within the FormWizard. FormWizard gives you lots of form choices to display your data any way you like. The closer your paper forms look to your Access forms, the easier it will be to enter data into the database from the paper forms that people give you.

Using FormWizard means that you only have to create a new form and tell Access what table you want to use with the form; FormWizard takes over from there. If FormWizard does not create the form exactly the way you want it to look, have no fear. You'll learn in Chapter 15, "How Do I Improve My Form's Appearance?" how to change the form.

Diving In

- Use forms to simulate the paper forms that people are used to.

- Use FormWizard to help you create forms.

● If you alter a record in form view, but then decide you don't want to make the change after all, select Edit Undo Current to remove the change.

Sunk

● Don't use a form if you need to display several records at once. A datasheet view suits that purpose better.

● Don't return to the database window to look at a datasheet view. Instead, click the datasheet view tool at the top of the form's toolbar.

Can I Print Data?

Use Access's Simple Printer Output

- Printing from the Datasheet   146
- Modifying the Output   148
- Printing from Forms   150

The screen is a fabulous output device, but many times only paper output will do. After entering several records, you might want to print a listing to double-check your data entry's accuracy. Access provides several ways to print the data in your database.

Part VII of this book explores some of the ways you can use Access to produce professional-looking reports. Before getting to that material, however, you need to be able to print simple listings of your data while you learn Access and enter data into your tables.

This chapter explains some of the simple ways to get a printed listing. Many Access developers find that a simple listing (versus a formatted in-depth report) is all they need for most of their work.

Printing from the Datasheet

You might recall from the end of Chapter 11, "Can I Manage Several Records?" that you can get a bird's-eye view of a datasheet by selecting File Print Preview while viewing the datasheet. The preview enables you to see how the datasheet would look on paper if you did print it.

  PSST!   Clicking the preview tool (the magnifying glass over the piece of paper) to request a preview is faster than using the menus.

Printing a datasheet onto paper is almost as easy as getting a preview on-screen. Open a datasheet view of the Tenant Data table, and prepare your printer for printing. The following steps will send the datasheet to your printer.

YIKES!

Be sure that your printer has paper and is online before trying to print something to it!

1. After retrieving the datasheet view, select File Print... from the menu. Access displays the Print dialog box shown in Figure 13.1.

Figure 13.1.

Getting ready to print a datasheet.

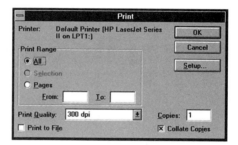

HMM...   Your Print dialog box might look a little different from the one shown in Figure 13.1 if your printer is not an HP LaserJet Series II.

2. Most of the time, you select File Print... to look at a single copy of your entire datasheet view. The default values shown in the dialog box are exactly right for a single copy of the datasheet. Therefore, press Enter (or click the OK button) to start the printing. Access prints the table in Tenant ID order because the Tenant ID field is the table's primary key.

YIKES!

The printed listing may not seem perfect, and it is not.
Most tables are too wide to print on a single sheet of
paper. Also, the Employer and Notes fields are not wide enough
to show all the data in them. Nevertheless, the printed listing is a
nice and quick way to get a preliminary copy of your table's data.

Modifying the Output

You can control several printing options from the Print dialog box.
Not only can you control the number of copies that are printed, but
you can control exactly which records and fields are printed as well.

Walk through the following steps to print the Tenant datasheet a
little differently:

1. Print a datasheet listing that includes only the Tenant ID,
    Tenant's Name, and Property ID fields. To start doing this,
    click and hold the mouse button over the Tenant ID field
    name (this highlights the field's name) in the datasheet view.
    Drag the mouse over the next two columns, and let up on
    the mouse button. Figure 13.2 shows what your datasheet
    should look like.

PSST!  Instead of limiting the fields, you can limit the records by
selecting only some of the records to print. Select records
from the row selector gray column at the left of the data.

Figure 13.2.

Selecting fields to print.

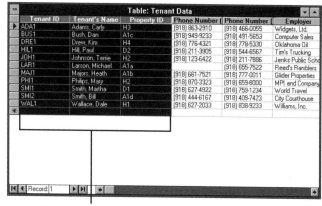

The selected records

YIKES!

You can first look at a print preview of the output, but the File Print Preview does not respect your selected fields. Preview always previews the entire printed table even if you select only some fields for printing to paper.

2. Select File Print to display the Print dialog box.

3. Change the Print Range to Selection. Doing so informs Access that you want to print only the fields that you selected rather than the entire table as would be done if you left All selected.

HMM...

If you print a large table, the table could take several pages of output. If you select Pages and enter the starting page number next to the From box and the ending page number next to the To box, Access prints only those pages rather than all the pages.

4. If your printer is capable of printing in *draft* mode or *letter quality* mode, you will be given the chance to select the mode in the Print Quality list box. If your printer's quality mode is rated in dots per inch, you'll be able to select the printed *DPI* value in the list. The larger the number, the better-looking your output will appear. Select the largest *DPI* value, or select *NLQ* if it is listed on your list box.

YIKES!

The lower the *DPI* value, the faster your datasheet will print but the worse it will look.

5. Next to the Copies box, enter 2 to print two copies.

    Most of the time, you'll want the Collate Copies box checked so that your multiple-page output collates properly. Leave the box checked.

6. If you want to print to a file rather than to your printer, check the Print to File box. For now, leave the box unchecked.

PSST!   If you have a nicer printer at a different location from your Access computer, print to a disk file and take the file (on a diskette) to the computer with the better printer, and use the DOS PRINT command to print the file.

7. Press Enter or select OK to start the printing.

Printing from Forms

Printing from a form is just as easy as printing a datasheet, but the output looks a lot different, because a form looks a lot different from

a datasheet. Printing form data takes a lot more paper than printing datasheet data. Use the following steps to print the data from the form view:

1. Close the datasheet view from the previous section's instructions with File Close.

2. Open the form named Tenant Form that you created in the preceding chapter.

3. When Access displays the first form, select File Preview to preview the printed forms. You'll see a screen like the one in Figure 13.3.

Figure 13.3.

A preview of the printed forms.

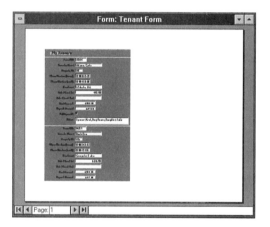

When the forms are printed, Access will not print one form per page. There are some advanced ways to control the number of forms per page, but you might be disappointed when printing the table from a form view.

4. Print the form. You can print directly from the preview by clicking the Print button. You'll see the familiar Print dialog box. Accept all the defaults and press Enter to get a printed listing of the form.

Chapter Wrap-Up

You now can print the data in datasheet view and form view. Preview your printed output before printing to make sure that Access is about to do what you want it to do. Whether you're in datasheet view or in form view, selecting File Print prints the data in the currently opened table.

Diving In

- Print your table after entering a lot of data to double-check your data's accuracy. *Garbage in produces garbage out,* according to a wise saying that Confucius might have written when debugging his abacus.

- Print from a datasheet view when you want to see a lot of records on each piece of paper.

- Print from a form view when you want to see forms printed, even though a lot of paper results from the printing.

Sunk

- Don't expect print preview to be able to print selected fields. The Access print preview system always shows you what the entire table would look like when printed even if you have selected only certain fields.

Part IV
Honing Your Skills

Can I Do More with a Datasheet?

Use Advanced Datasheet Commands

- Finding a Needle in the Stack of Data   156
- Replacing Data   159
- Hiding Fields   161
- Format Your Data   162
- One Last Datasheet Change...   164

Now that you've seen how to create tables, edit with datasheets, create and use forms, and print some data, it is time to hone some of your skills further. This chapter takes a closer look at some of the things you can do to make working in the datasheet view easier.

You will learn how to search for data, replace data, and hide columns, as well as all sorts of other goodies that make your datasheet viewing more productive.

Finding a Needle in the Stack of Data

Because our sample database, which contains only Laura Landlady's Tenant table so far, is extremely small, this chapter's searching exercises may seem trivial. With only a handful of records, you can more easily find data with your eyes when you want to see a certain record. Nevertheless, the searching techniques that you learn about here work just as well if there are 10,000 records in the file rather than only a few.

PSST!  If you have used a Windows word processor before, you'll find that the Access find and replace features work just like they do in your word processor.

When you want to find a specific data item, you can have Access find the data for you. You can limit the find to a specific field and require that Access respect or ignore the uppercase and lowercase differences between the data that Access finds and the data you're searching for.

Open the datasheet view for the Tenant table. The following steps walk you through a search for the letters *MPI*:

1. Select Edit Find... from the menu. Access displays the Find dialog box shown in Figure 14.1.

Figure 14.1.

The Find dialog box.

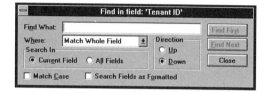

PSST!   The binoculars tool is the shortcut for selecting Edit Find... .

2. Type MPI in the Find What box.

3. Click the Where list's down arrow to display a list of search choices. Select Any Part of Field so that Access looks for *MPI* anywhere it appears in any field rather than only at the beginning of a field. The Match Whole Field option is useful only if you want the matched record to contain a field with *only* the letters *MPI*.

4. When you began the search, the first record under the Tenant ID field was highlighted. Access assumes that you want the search to be limited to the field that was highlighted when you issued the Find command. If you want the search to span all the fields (and in this case you do), click the All Fields option of the Search In box.

5. The search always begins at the record highlighted when you issued the Find command. Depending on the Direction option, Access searches all records Down from the current

record or Up from the current record. In this example, you want Access to search from the current record (the first one) down into the table, so make sure the Down Direction is selected.

HMM... If you selected Match Case, Access would find only those records that contained the uppercase letters *MPI*, whereas if the Match Case option was not selected, Access would find records with any of the following combinations of *MPI*: *MPI, mpi, Mpi, mPi, mpI, mPI*. Because the letters *MPI* appear in the Tenant table only once, the Match Case option is moot here, and you can leave it alone.

YIKES!
The Search Fields as Formatted option slows down a search and is useful only when you want to search formatted data in a particular field using formatted data. You cannot select this option if you are searching across all fields as you are doing here.

6.   Press Enter to select Find First, and Access will begin the search. The Find dialog box will *not* go away when Access finds the record. The row selector column's arrow will be pointing to the record containing the found value, however. If there were several occurrences of *MPI*, you could press Find Next to find the next one.

7.   Press Esc to get rid of the Find dialog box, and you'll see that Access highlighted the letters *MPI* in the found record.

Skip This, It's Technical

If you are familiar with the DOS wildcard characters * and ?, you can use them inside your search data. For example, a*c finds *ac, a c, abc, a83939c, abb^4d/bbbc,* and so on, whereas a?c finds *aac, abc, acc, a4c,* and so on.

Replacing Data

Replacing data values with other data values is simple. You might want to replace all occurrences of St. with Saint or Mac with Mc. If there are several hundred records in your database, changing each one by hand is tedious and does not lend itself well to a computerized database system. You bought Access to do tedious work for you.

The following steps guide you through changing all the phone-number area codes from 918 to 750:

1. Click the Tenant ID field of the first record to make it the current record.

2. Select Edit Replace... and Access responds by displaying the Replace dialog box shown in Figure 14.2.

Notice that the text searched for earlier is next to the Find What box. Access is trying to help you by saving some typing on your part. The problem is that you don't want to change the text you searched for earlier.

Figure 14.2.

The Replace dialog box.

3.   Type 918 next to Find What, and press Tab. The Find What box is the text to find, and the Replace With box will contain the change you want to make.

4.   Type 750 next to the Replace With box.

5.   Leave the Search In option set to All Fields so that the entire database is searched. Leave the Match Case field alone because there are no uppercase or lowercase letters to match in this search-and-replace operation. If you were to click the Replace button (don't do so), Access would find the first occurrence of 918 and ask whether you wanted it changed. Don't, however, click Replace because we want to replace *all* the 918s with 750s. Click Replace All to instruct Access to replace all occurrences of 918 with 750.

When finished, Access displays a dialog box telling you that Access has reached the end of the *dynaset.*

YIKES!

You've never heard of the word *dynaset;* how dare Access tell you something like that! Dynaset is a fancy name for all the records found that met your search criteria. You'll read a lot more about dynasets in Chapter 16, "What Is a Query?"

6.   Click OK. Access displays yet another dialog box, shown in Figure 14.3. Access is letting you know that you cannot undo the replacement after you click OK. That's fine, so click OK or press Enter.

Figure 14.3.

Access warns you about making the replacements permanent.

7. Press Esc to get rid of the Replace dialog box, and you'll see that the changes are made.

 PSST! The find and replace commands are also available from within any form view.

Hiding Fields

There might be some fields on the screen that you want to keep in the table but not show on the datasheet view. You can hide a column from the datasheet view without deleting the column from the table by following these steps:

1. Scroll to the right of the datasheet until the Date Moved Out column comes into view.

2. Click the field name so that the entire Date Moved Out column is highlighted.

3. Select Layout Hide Columns, and Access hides the selected column from view.

HMM... The column hiding lasts only as long as you are in the current datasheet view. If you were to return to the database window and select the Tenant Data table datasheet view again, the Date Moved Out column would be back.

If you want to show the hidden column again, select Layout Show Columns... and you'll see the scrolling list of field names shown in Figure 14.4. Every field with a check mark will be displayed, and every field without a check mark is hidden. To make a field reappear, put the check mark back by highlighting the field name and clicking the Show button.

Figure 14.4.

Hiding a column from the datasheet view.

A hidden field ——

Format Your Data

Almost all the data types come with preselected formats. For instance, if you do not specify another format, a date field always displays in the familiar *mm/dd/yy* format you've been seeing. Currency fields always display with a dollar sign and two decimal places, and so on.

Although extended field formatting is way beyond the scope of this book, you should take a few moments while looking at the datasheet to consider your fields' formats. Most of the time, the default format selected by Access works fine. You have probably had no problem understanding the format of any of the Tenant Data table's data. However, just for practice, you should see how to change a field's format in case you do want a different look for your datasheet (and form) fields.

The datasheet design view's Field Properties (remember the datasheet design view?) determines how a field's contents will appear when displayed. The following steps change the Date Moved In field from the *mm/dd/yy* format to *dayOfWeekName*,

monthName, day, year (called the *Long Date format*). In other words, 8/12/93 becomes Thursday, August 12, 1993.

YIKES!

Be careful about getting carried away. Some formats, such as this Long Date format, can be extremely wide, and you won't be able to see all the data in the field unless you widen the field's column in the datasheet view.

1. Click the datasheet design view tool (the leftmost tool).

2. Click the Date Moved In record (anywhere on the record or in the row selector field to the left).

3. Click the Format box inside the Field Properties pane. A down arrow appears next to the box indicating that a selection list is available for that format.

4. Click the down arrow, and you'll see a list of Date/Time formats from which you can choose.

5. Select Long Date and press Enter.

6. Click the datasheet view tool (the second tool from the left). Access warns you that you haven't saved the table's changes (the format changes). Click OK to indicate that you want the changes saved.

    Access displays the datasheet, and the Date Moved In's data is spelled out in the Long Date format. Widen the field so that you can see all the data.

7. Now, put the format *back* where it was! You'll get tired of having that wide field around in these examples. Be sure to save the table after you reformat the Date Moved In field to Short Date again.

One Last Datasheet Change...

Here's a quickie that you might like. You can get rid of the separating lines that box in a datasheet's data by selecting Layout Grid-lines. The lines will disappear. You can put them back by selecting Layout Gridlines again.

PSST!  When you hide the gridlines on-screen, the lines won't appear when you print the datasheet either.

Chapter Wrap-Up

This chapter gave instructions for some of the most useful data-changing commands you will need. You learned how to find data and how to search for data. Finding and searching requires that you match uppercase and lowercase or else ignore the case of your searched data. Finding and searching requires that you specify the find and search direction, specify which fields to use, and tell Access whether you want the first occurrence or all occurrences of the found data to be used.

The opposite of finding data is hiding it! You can use Layout Hide and Layout Show to hide or show any field you want in the datasheet view. Often, when you are viewing a datasheet, the columns that you are least interested in at the time are getting in your way. Hiding those columns makes your tour in the datasheet easier but still maintains the original data in the table itself.

Diving In

- Use Access to find one or all occurrences of a value.

- Let Access do all the tedious searching and replacing of data.

- Hide whatever fields you don't want to see in datasheet view.

- Hide the gridlines from the datasheet if you want.

Sunk

- Don't forget to select All Fields when finding and replacing for data that might appear in one of several fields. If you know the field to look in, however, selecting Current Field will speed your searching.

How Do I Improve My Form's Appearance?

By Customizing Your Forms

- *Always Start with FormWizard*   168
- *Working with the Form Design*   169
- *Changing the Form's Colors*   170
- *Changing the Form's Field Locations*   172
- *Changing the Form's Field Sizes*   175

At the end of the preceding chapter, you learned how to change the format of certain data in a datasheet view. You have now learned all about rearranging, resizing, and reformatting a datasheet view so that your data is displayed just the way you like it.

You can rearrange, resize, and reformat your form's data as well. Just because you used FormWizard to create a form doesn't mean that Access keeps you from changing the form's appearance. This chapter explores some of the ways to personalize your form so that its appearance is the way you like it.

Always Start with FormWizard

There are a lot of messy details involved with designing a form that FormWizard protects you from. Rarely if ever should you attempt to design a form without the help of FormWizard. If you need a very specific form that looks unlike any of the forms available in FormWizard, use FormWizard to design a base form that you can then modify to look the way you want it to look.

 HMM...   The form design view is the view from which you modify a form's layout, just as the table's design view is where you modify a table's layout.

The rest of this chapter gives you a sample of some of the things you can do with a form's design. An entire book could be devoted to form design and to the tools supplied with Access that enable you to design forms. Luckily, you rarely if ever should need a form that looks much different from the ones FormWizard creates for you.

PSST!    If you have ever worked with Visual Basic, you'll find that the form design view has almost identical tools and menus.

Working with the Form Design

Open the Tenant Form, and look at the first record's data. The toolbar contains the tools you are already familiar with. Click the leftmost tool (the form design view tool) to change to the form design view. Enlarge the form design view to full-screen by double-clicking the form window's title bar, and you'll see the screen shown in Figure 15.1.

Figure 15.1.

Looking at the form's design view.

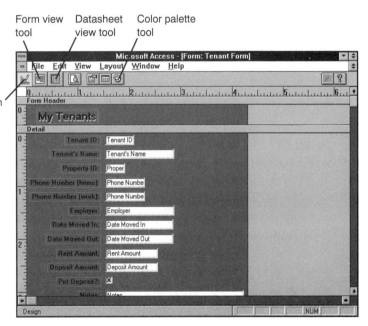

The text in the white field boxes is *not* data from the table. Look closer and you'll see that the table's field names reside where the data normally goes in the form.

PSST! Pay special attention to the toolbar names labelled in Figure 15.1 because the rest of this chapter refers to them by name.

A form has three parts, called *bands:* a header band, a detail band, and a footer band. The header band contains the form's title (named by you when you created the form originally with FormWizard). This band appears at the top of the first form displayed or printed. The form's detail band contains the data from the form. The footer band contains text and controls and appears only *after* all forms are displayed or printed (FormWizard did nothing with the footer band).

HMM... You don't have to have a header or a footer band. Both are optional.

Each part of a form is called a *control.* The title is a control, the field names are controls, and the boxes that display the table's data are controls.

Changing the Form's Colors

You might not like the color selection that FormWizard chose. The color palette tool enables you to change colors with a mouse click. Follow these steps to change the header band and detail band to different colors:

1. Click anywhere within the blank space on the header band to highlight the Form Header title bar. (Don't click the title itself.)

2. Click the color palette tool. You'll see the color palette, like the one shown in Figure 15.2.

Figure 15.2.

Looking at the color palette view.

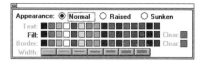

The palette's first, third, and fourth row descriptions (Text, Border, and Width) are grayed out because you can control only the fill color of a header's background area (the fill color is the background color).

3. Click one of the colors in the Fill row. Select bright red (Laura Landlady's favorite color). When you click red, the background in the header band changes to show you the result.

4. Click the title My Tenants and watch how the color palette changes. Now, all four rows in the palette are active. Clicking the first row's palette changes the text color, clicking the second changes the background, clicking the third changes the border around the title, and clicking the fourth row's palette changes the width of the line around the control. Select some snazzy colors for the title that look OK against the red background.

   You will find that even when you select a fill and border color, the title doesn't seem to change. Deselect the Clear boxes to the right of the Fill and Border color rows. The Clear boxes keep the background and text colors the same as those of the surrounding area unless you uncheck the boxes. Now, the title takes on the colors you selected.

5. Leave the palette displayed, but click anywhere within the detail band's blank area. Change the color of the detail. Yellow ought to really stand out under that red heading band!

6. Double-click the palette's control box (the control box is small, but there is one in the palette's upper-left corner) to close the palette.

YIKES!

Don't follow Laura's strange red-and-yellow color scheme for your own forms. Too many colors make the form look too busy and take away from the importance of the data.

PSST!  You can change the colors of the data boxes themselves, but leave them white with black letters for this database.

HMM... At any time during the form design, you can click the form view tool (the second from the left) to see what the finished form (with data) will look like. Switch back to form design view by clicking the far-left tool.

Changing the Form's Field Locations

You can rearrange the location of the fields in your forms. The following steps will show you how to move the Phone Number (work) field to the right of the Phone Number (home) field.

HMM... The FormWizard created a form with one field per line (that's the meaning of the Single-Column form you selected in FormWizard). Sometimes, a table has so many fields that you'll want to move some fields side-by-side to make more fields fit on a single screen.

1. Be careful to do this exactly as described: Click and hold down that click while the mouse cursor is over the title for the Phone Number (work) field. You'll see the cursor change to a hand shape. The hand indicates that you are grabbing the field and are about to move it.

2. Move the hand until it rests to the right of the Phone Number (home) data box. Leave about an inch between the Phone Number (home) field's data box and the Phone Number (work) field's title. The end of the box you are moving will extend outside the form's boundaries, but that's OK. Let go of the mouse button, and your screen should look like the one in Figure 15.3. If you don't think you moved the field far enough to the right, move it some more.

Figure 15.3.

Moving a field.

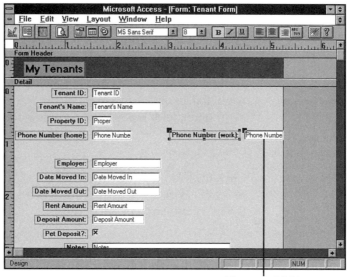

You might have thought that you were moving only the field's title, but as you can see, you moved the title and the data. The form widened a bit to hold the longer line. The only problem is that a big blank line is left in the field's original position.

3. Click the lower arrow on the vertical scroll bar once so that the detail band is in full view and the header band is scrolled off the screen.

4. Move the mouse cursor to the left side of the form, just above the Employer field title, so that the cursor sits somewhere in the blank area.

5. Click and hold the mouse button while moving the mouse cursor to the lower-right corner of the form (until the mouse cursor falls under and to the right of the Notes field). As you move the mouse, you are dragging a box along with you.

6. Let go of the mouse when the box encloses the bottom seven fields. You just created a box that groups all those fields together.

7. Place the cursor somewhere in the middle of the box, and click once without releasing the mouse button. The cursor becomes a hand again.

8. Drag the box up, and you'll see that the fields and their associated data move with the box. You can release the box when the lower seven fields fall just below the Phone Number (home) field. You've just closed up the blank line left by the field you moved earlier. Your screen will look like the one in Figure 15.4.

9. Click the form view to see what the resulting form really looks like. You'll see that the form looks more balanced with the two phone numbers side-by-side.

PSST!   Use the ruler guides at the left and top of the form to align the fields at the same horizontal position.

Figure 15.4.

Bringing the other fields up.

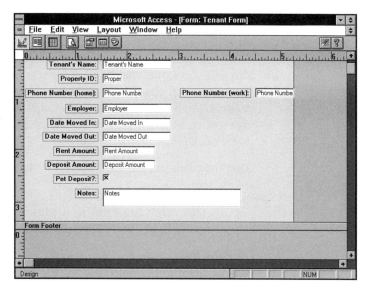

YIKES!

Don't think that you changed the table or data in any way. You just adjusted the form, not the data underneath. The table's structure and its data are independent of any form's appearance.

Changing the Form's Field Sizes

The phone number fields aren't wide enough to display their contents properly. Instead of moving those fields, you need to resize them as explained here:

1. Display the form design view if it is not currently displayed.

2. Click the Phone Number (home) field's data control once.

3. Move the cursor to one of the corners at the right of the box. The cursor will change to a double-pointing arrow. (If the cursor is the hand shape, keep moving the cursor to one of the right corners until it changes shape.) The arrows indicate that you can now resize the box.

4. Drag the corner to the right about one-half inch until you can see the entire field name.

5. Repeat steps 2 through 4 for the next field's box so that you can see its full field name, Phone Number (work), in its box.

6. Click the form view, and you'll see the results of your labor. Both phone number fields are wide enough to hold their data values.

7. Save your form (File Close Yes) so that Access will remember your adjustments.

Skip This, It's Technical

If you wanted to design a form from scratch, laying out each field, each field's title, the form's title, and all the rest of the form's elements and controls, you could do so. Most of us don't have time to waste, however, and editing a form created by FormWizard is usually much faster than designing a form from scratch.

Chapter Wrap-Up

This chapter showed you how to take a form created by FormWizard and modify the form to look the way you want. Most forms will come out of FormWizard looking great, but you still may need to move or resize certain columns to achieve the look you require.

The form design view is the place to change a form. While in the form design view, you can change colors by displaying the color palette, and you can move and resize fields by clicking and dragging.

Diving In

- Click the form's design view tool to enter the form design view.

- Use the hand cursor to move fields and their data controls.

- Use the double-arrow cursor to resize controls on your form.

Sunk

- Don't design a form from scratch. Doing so takes too much time. Use FormWizard and then change the form to suit your needs.

Part V
Querying the Database

What Is a Query?

A Query Is Just a Database Question

- *Building a Query*   182
- *Preparing for the Query*   183
- *Selecting Fields*   184
- *Asking the Query*   186

A *query* is just a question you ask your database. Access does not understand English, so you must ask your question in a structured manner. As with most elements of Access, the graphical interface walks you through the creation of a query so that Access can return the answers you request.

A query is an *object*, just as a table and a form are objects. You might not think of a question as being an object at first, but you can store queries just like you can store data. Don't you often ask the same question more than once?

HMM... When you use Find to look for data, you have to repeat the same command every time you want to find the same records. After building a query to search for data, you can tell Access to follow the instructions in the stored query.

Queries are much more powerful searching tools than the Find menu options that you are already familiar with. Instead of finding a record that contains a field value equal to the one you are looking for, a query enables you to find records that meet strenuous criteria, such as "List all my tenants who pay less than $400 rent," "List our customers who bought 20 or more products and who live in the 55555 ZIP code," and "List every female student in our student database who is enrolled in a business course, is married, and is between 21 and 65." Questions like these would be difficult if data were still kept in filing cabinets rather than in computers.

Building a Query

The first query that we'll create will be a simple data-viewing query. The datasheet views that you have been seeing are too wide, and most of the fields are rarely needed. You may use a query to display fewer fields as the following sections do.

Preparing for the Query

The following steps walk you through the creation of a query that displays the Tenant's Name and Phone Number (home), in alphabetical order, so that Laura Landlady can look at an up-to-date phone list of her tenants:

1. Return to the database window in the Tenants database if you are not there already.

2. Click the Query button. There are no queries in the current database because you haven't added any.

3. Select the New button, and you'll see the Add Table window, shown in Figure 16.1.

Figure 16.1.

Select a table for the query.

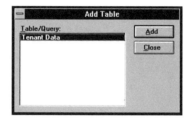

Because there is only one table so far in the database, only one table is listed in the Add Table window. A query must have data to work on, so you must tell the query what table to use. Press Enter to select Add.

4. If there were more tables to choose from, you could also add them to the query. A query can be applied to more than one table. This database has only one table so far, so select Close to close the Add Table window.

Access displays the Select Query window, shown in Figure 16.2. The top pane describes the table (Tenant Data) that the query will use. If you had selected more than one table in step 3, more tables would be listed in the top pane.

YIKES!

The query definition window is a little strange-looking, but you'll understand its features before this chapter is done.

Figure 16.2.

Building a query from the Select Query window.

Tables field list box

Query definition area

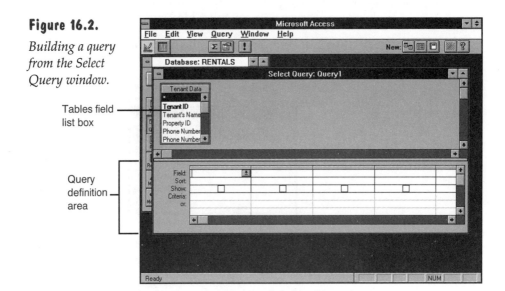

Selecting Fields

The lower pane in the Select Query window is ready for the rest of our question. The first part of our question began with "Given the Tenant Data table,..." You now must supply the specifics of what you want from the Tenant Data table. Follow these steps to specify the tenant's name and home phone number fields:

1. The Tenant Data table window in the upper pane contains a list of all the fields in the Tenant Data table. Instead of remembering and typing field names in the query, you only have to drag the names from the table to the query in the lower pane.

   You can drag the names from the table to the query, or if you double-click each name, Access will drag the name for you. Therefore, double-click the Tenant's Name field. Access drops the field into the first box of the lower pane.

 HMM... You could have dragged the field name to the lower pane, but why not let Access do the work?

PSST!  You can grab the right edge of the Tenant Table window and drag it to the right to make the table wider so that you can read all its field names.

2. Click the Sort box under the Tenant's Name box in the lower pane. A down arrow appears. Click the down arrow to see a list of sort options.

HMM... *Sorting* means that you want to put data in some kind of order. There are *ascending sorts* (from low to high data values) and *descending sorts* (from high to low). If you sort a list of names, you are alphabetizing them. If you sort a list of numbers, you are putting them in numerical sequence.

Select the Ascending option under the Tenant's Name field. You are telling Access that you want this query to display tenants' names in alphabetical order from *A* to *Z*.

PSST!   The reason you typed the tenant's last name followed by the first name in earlier chapters was to ensure that the names would sort properly.

YIKES!

If you don't specify a sort for the query, Access displays the result of the query in the primary key order (the Tenant ID in this case), even if the primary key field is not part of the query.

3. Double-click the Phone Number (home) field. Access sends the Phone Number (home) field to the second column in the lower pane. Your screen should look something like the one in Figure 16.3.

4. Save the query by double-clicking the Select Query's control button in the window's upper-left corner. When Access prompts you for a query name, type `Phonebook Query`.

Asking the Query

There are several ways to run the query you just created. One of the more straightforward methods is to select the query in the database window and select Open. Do that now, and you'll see a datasheet view of the phonebook.

Figure 16.3.

Your screen after you specify the query.

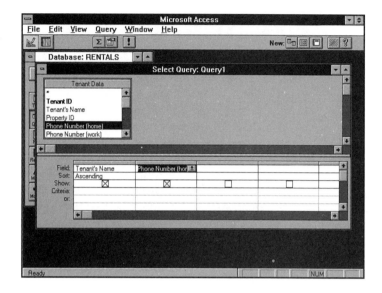

PSST!   Resize the query's resulting data by dragging the right edge of the field names to the right.

The result of a query is called a *dynaset*. A dynaset is a subset of the table's data. After you retrieve a dynaset from a query, you can view the dynaset's data in a form or datasheet view as if it were a regular table.

Skip This, It's Technical

Access uses a series of data pointers when displaying a dynaset. When you view a dynaset, you are actually looking at the underlying table's data through a series of pointers to the data. When you change data in a dynaset, you are actually telling Access which pointed-to data to manipulate in the original table.

Chapter Wrap-Up

A query is nothing more than a question that you ask about your database. This chapter walked you through the creation of a simple query that displayed a subset of the Tenant Data table. Often, you are not interested in looking at all the fields when viewing a datasheet; the dynaset (subset) produced with the query keeps unwanted fields from getting in the way.

Fun Fact
Unlike competing products, Access shows active data in queries. Changing the dynaset changes the underlying table data. The term dynaset *means* dynamic subset *(a changing subset of your data).*

Create a query by clicking the Query button in the database window. The query's design is achieved by pointing and clicking table names and sort orders so that the query's resulting dynaset behaves properly.

Diving In

● Use queries to ask questions of your database.

● Build your queries from the Query button in the database window.

● Select a sorting method if you want the query's dynaset to be displayed or printed in a certain order.

Sunk

● Don't forget that resulting data from a query (the dynaset's data) is live data from the database table. If you change the data, you are changing not a copy of the data, but the values in the original table.

What More Can I Do with Queries?

Use Relational Operators

- Meeting Your Match   190
- Extending the Criteria   193

Queries can be more powerful than the simple one you saw in the preceding chapter. You can use a query to limit the data displayed so that only certain values appear in the dynaset (and you can eliminate certain values from the dynaset too).

This chapter delves more deeply into the query's definition and shows you how to add power to your data selections.

Meeting Your Match

Suppose you were looking for every record in your table that matched a certain value. You could just perform the menu's Find command. But building a search instead will enable you to see the resulting data records in both a datasheet view and a form view and will enable you to save the query for later execution.

In the Tenant table, there are three people who pay $300 in rent each month. With only a few records, finding the three records is easy to do, but let's create a query that does the searching for you. You then can save the query to request it any time you want the same selected records.

HMM...   We're asking this query: "Which tenants pay exactly $300 a month?"

Unlike the preceding chapter's query, this query should not display all the fields used by the query. In other words, it would be redundant to list the rent field of the queried records because all the fields will be the same ($300). You can query on a field but not necessarily display the field in the query's result, as shown in these steps:

1. Create a new query by selecting New after clicking Query in the database window.

Access displays the Add Table window that you saw in the preceding chapter, with one exception: the query you created from the preceding chapter is in the window along with the Tenant Data table. When you use an existing query inside another query, you are in effect using that query's resulting dynaset.

2.   Select the Tenant Data table, and click Add to add the Tenant table to the query you are building.

3.   Close the Add Table window.

4.   Double-click Tenant's Name to send it to the first query's field.

5.   Click Sort and select Ascending as you did in the preceding chapter.

6.   Double-click Rent Amount to move that field name from the Tenant Data table of fields to the query.

7.   Click the box in the third row of the query area (the row labeled Show). The x inside the box disappears.

The Rent Amount field will still be used in the query, but it will not appear in the final dynaset. Only the Tenant's Name field will appear in the dynaset.

8.   Click the Criteria row under the Rent Amount column, and type 300 in the box. Your screen should look like the one in Figure 17.1.

Figure 17.1.

After you are done creating the new query.

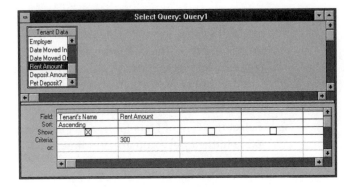

PSST!   You are telling Access that this query is to use the Tenant's Name field and the Rent Amount field. The query is successful only if the rent amount is equal to $300. If the rent amount is equal to $300, the query should display that tenant's name but not the rent.

9. Save the query by selecting File Close, and name the query
    `Rent 300 Query`.

10. Execute the query by selecting the `Rent 300 Query` query and then Open. A dynaset appears for the three renters who pay exactly $300 in rent.

PSST!   If you are searching for a match based on a text field, you can use either uppercase or lowercase letters. The query does not look at the case of letters when making a match.

Extending the Criteria

There are times when you want to query your data but a simple match won't do. For example, what if Laura Landlady wanted a list of all her tenants who pay $300 *or less* in rent? Table 17.1 lists the Access *relational operators* that you must learn in order to write more powerful queries.

Table 17.1. The relational operators.

Operator	Meaning
>	Greater than
<	Less than
>=	Greater than or equal to
<=	Less than or equal to
<>	Not equal to
=	Equal to (not needed for simple matches)

Skip This, It's Technical

If you are familiar with the DOS wildcard characters * and ?, you can use them in your searches. You can also use the Access wildcard # to search a position for a numeric digit (whereas the ? compares against any character, numeric or otherwise). If you use a wildcard, Access adds the word like in front of it and surrounds the search criteria in quotation marks. Therefore, a*c becomes like "a*c". Access is funny that way.

Fun Fact
*The author
(me!) has
always had a
hard time
remembering
in which
direction the
less than and
greater than
symbols point.
Think of each
symbol as an
open mouth
that wants to
eat the bigger
amount.*

If you wanted to look for a certain tenant who pays $300 or less in rent, you would use <= 300 in the Criteria box. If you wanted to find all tenants who moved in after 12/1/92, you would enter >12/1/92 under a Date Moved In field in the query.

The following steps produce a query based on the selections just described. In other words, this query creates a dynaset of data records that answers this question: "What are the people's names who pay $300 or less a month in rent and who moved in after 12/1/92?"

1. Open a new query based on the Tenant table. Double-click to bring down the Tenant's Name, and request an ascending sort as you have done before.

2. Double-click the Date Moved In field name. Leave the box checked so that this field shows in the dynaset created by this query.

3. In the Date Moved In's Criteria box, type >12/1/92.

YIKES!

Look what Access did! Access put a pound sign around the date, turning it into this: >#12/1/92#. That's the format Access prefers. You could have typed the date like that, but why should you when Access changes it for you?

4. Double-click the Rent Amount field to bring it into the query. Uncheck the Show box, and type this as the criteria: <=300. Your screen will look like the one in Figure 17.2.

Figure 17.2.

A relational query.

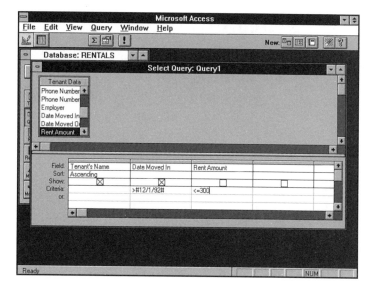

5. Save the query under the name Date and Rent Check, and run the query. Access displays the four records in the table that match this relational query.

HMM... As with most features of Access, this query is not really fantastic with only a few records to choose from. However, if the table had 40,000 records, the query would still work!

Chapter Wrap-Up

You've now learned to extend your querying power by specifying queries with relational criteria. You can now look for all records that meet a certain relational result. Using the greater than, less than, equal to, and other relational operators, you've turned Access into your slave that finds data which falls between the cracks of the relations you set up.

Diving In

- Use relational queries to increase your querying power.

- Add several fields with relational criteria to narrow down your table queries to very specific answers.

Sunk

- Don't be surprised if Access changes your criteria a bit by adding pound signs or quotation marks.

- Don't worry about making uppercase and lowercase matches in your query criteria because Access does not distinguish between them.

How Do Queries Work with Forms?

Forms and Complex Queries Go Well Together!

- *Combining Relations: The Logical Operators* 198
- *The AND Operator* 199
- *Using BETWEEN* 200
- *The OR Operator* 200
- *One More Major Query Step* 201
- *Linking a Form to a Query* 205

Both of the preceding chapters showed you how to create queries. All the queries' resulting dynasets, however, were seen only in the datasheet view. You read that you can use queries in form view also, but you didn't see how to combine forms and queries.

This chapter extends the power of forms by showing you how to view a dynaset (a query's result) inside a form. A short detour is taken to extend your working knowledge of queries so that they include the relational operations you learned in the preceding chapter. After you build a complex query, we'll use that query in a new form. People who know little about Access, but who have to use the database application that you create, enjoy working with forms more than with datasheet views.

PSST!   Keep in mind that the query's resulting dynaset is like a miniature table that you can use as if it were a stand-alone table.

Combining Relations: The Logical Operators

There are other operators that make your queries work harder for you. You learned in the preceding chapter how to make queries perform relational tests on field values. It's easy to view records that are less than, or equal to, or greater than certain values. Some relational tests, however, require a combination of relational operators. That's where the AND, BETWEEN, and OR operators (sometimes called *logical operators*) come into play.

The AND Operator

What if you want to test to see whether a value falls within a certain range? For example, what if you wanted to see a list of renters who pay between $250 and $325?

YIKES!

The relational operators by themselves cannot handle range testing of values. Neither >$250 nor <$325 by itself will test to see whether a value falls between those two numbers.

The AND operator is needed to test for a range of values. AND does not look like an operator, but it is. AND works just as it does in English. For example, here is how you would ask the rental range question:

"Which tenants pay more than $250 in rent and less than $325?"

See the AND in the sentence? AND goes between two other relational operators to check for a range of values like this:

```
>250 AND <325
```

HMM... Access does not care whether you use uppercase or lowercase letters for the AND operator. Both AND and and are the same.

If you wanted to test for those tenants who pay between $250 and $325, you could specify a range-inclusive relational test like this:

```
>=250 AND <=325
```

YIKES!

Remember that you are still learning more about the query definition window's Criteria box. The more powerful criteria that Access enables you to specify, the more you can zero in on the records that you want to work with or report on.

Using BETWEEN

If you understand AND, BETWEEN is even easier. BETWEEN replaces an AND for inclusive range testing. BETWEEN is easier to use than AND, because a BETWEEN test reads more like its English equivalent. The following lines are equal to each other:

```
>=250 AND <=325
```

and

```
BETWEEN 250 AND 325
```

Fun Fact
If you ever learn Access Basic or another programming language, you'll be glad you mastered AND and OR. Every major programming language uses the relational operators AND and OR in the same way that this chapter does.

The OR Operator

Use OR when you have to test fields that might be one of several different values. For example, you might want to find everybody who moved in the first day of a quarter. Putting OR between two values in a criterion selects records that meet *either* of the criteria. As with AND, the OR operator reads just like its spoken counterpart. Instead of saying

   "What tenants moved in on 1/1/93 or 4/1/93 or 7/1/93 or 10/1/93?"

you would specify the criteria in Access like this:

```
1/1/93 OR 4/1/93 OR 7/1/93 OR 10/1/93
```

One More Major Query Step

The final step in using relational operators is to spread them across more than one field if you want to. For instance, let's combine *both* of the preceding sections' query criteria into one complex query that reads like this:

> *"What are the names of the tenants who pay between $250 and $325 or moved in on the date of a new quarter?"*

Notice the *or*. In other words, we want to see those tenants who pay rent within the dollar range no matter when they moved in. Also, we want to see those tenants who moved in on a quarter's starting date no matter how much they pay in rent.

YIKES!

If you don't think your database needs will be anything like Laura Landlady's, think again (I mean that with all due respect). Combining search criteria in your queries is one of the most important skills you will master, but mastering relational operators does take time unless you've used them in other programs before Access. Here are just some of the many query-like questions you might find yourself asking:

> *"What customers bought more than $1,000 in goods last year and paid cash?"*

> *"Who are the vendors we bought from more than four times last year and to whom we paid over $5,000?"*

> *"Which inventory items are getting low (fewer than three items in stock) and sell more than five units a year?"*

Create the complex query described previously by following the steps given next. You'll see how the Access query system (called

Query By Example, or *QBE,* because of the point-and-click nature of the query definition window) spreads the OR operator across fields for you.

1. Open a new query from the database window.

2. Add the Tenant Data table to the query, and close the Add Table window.

3. Double-click the Tenant's name field, and specify a Sort Ascending option in the lower pane.

4. Double-click the Date Moved In field to bring it into the query's lower pane.

5. In the Criteria box, type this:

   ```
   1/1/93 Or 4/1/93 Or 7/1/93 Or 10/1/93
   ```

   As is common in a query's Criteria box, Access changes your typing just a little by putting pound signs around each date.

6. Double-click the Rent Amount field to bring it into the query's lower pane.

HMM... If you wanted the Rent Amount to appear first in the resulting dynaset, you would add the Rent Amount field to the query *before* adding the Date Moved In field. The same records would be selected, but their field order would be rearranged.

YIKES!
Be careful here! You must follow the next instruction exactly.

7. Move the cursor to the Rent Amount's line below the first Criteria line (the one whose row name reads Or:). Type the following information into that box:

BETWEEN 250 AND 325

Make sure your query looks like the one shown in Figure 18.1.

Figure 18.1.

Performing OR across fields.

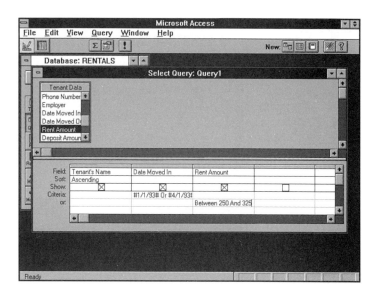

PSST!

If you had given any other field a criterion on the *same* row as the first criterion, an AND operation would be performed. If you want Access to relate two different field values with OR, the fields' criteria must go on separate lines. The row's title Or: before the Criteria line is there to remind you of this fact. If both criteria had been next to each other, here is the question you would be asking:

"Who are the tenants who pay between $250 and $325 and who moved in on the date of a new quarter?"

No tenants would meet this strict criteria.

8. Save the query under the name Qtrly Rent Range Query.

9. Execute the query by clicking the Open button. You'll see the datasheet view shown in Figure 18.2.

Figure 18.2.

Executing the complex query.

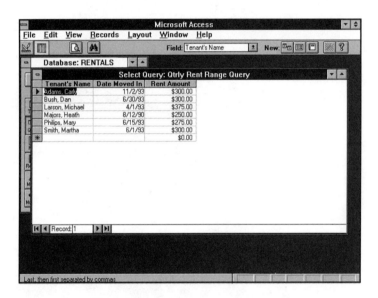

Tenant's Name	Date Moved In	Rent Amount
Adams, Carly	11/2/93	$300.00
Bush, Dan	6/30/93	$300.00
Larson, Michael	4/1/93	$375.00
Majors, Heath	8/12/90	$250.00
Philips, Mary	6/15/93	$275.00
Smith, Martha	6/1/93	$300.00
*		$0.00

HMM...   There is only one tenant who paid on a quarter's beginning (Michael Larson). His rent did not fall within the rent range, but the date he moved in triggered his inclusion in this dynaset.

10. Close the datasheet. The next section will create a form that uses this query.

Linking a Form to a Query

Now that you've got a form that takes advantage of the relational operators, it is time to combine that query's resulting dynaset into a nice form view.

The following steps use FormWizards to create a form from the Qtrly Rent Range Query query. Creating a form from a query is just as easy as creating a form from a table—after all, a query's resulting dynaset is just a different table view of data. Here are the steps you should follow to create the form:

1. Click the Form button, and select New.

2. At the Select A Table/Query list box, select (by first clicking the down arrow) Qtrly Rent Range Query.

3. Press the FormWizard button, and FormWizards displays the form selection screen. For this form, select Tabular and click OK.

PSST! A tabular form looks a little like a datasheet with better-looking controls.

4. Highlight the Tenant's Name field, and click >. Highlight the Rent Amount (not the Date Moved In) field, and click >. Finally, highlight Date Moved In, and click >. Even though the query's dynaset produces the fields in a different order from this new form's order, you control the form's order by selecting the fields here on this screen.

5. Select Next. When asked to select a kind of form, click Shadowed and select Next.

6. Type the title Mid-Price and Quarterly Renters, and click the Open button. Access creates the form and displays it on-screen as shown in Figure 18.3. The form looks nice, doesn't it?

Figure 18.3.

Looking at the finished query-based form.

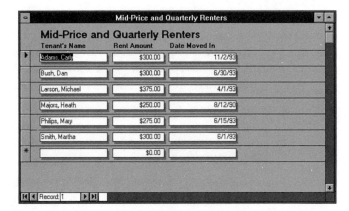

Mid-Price and Quarterly Renters		
Mid-Price and Quarterly Renters		
Tenant's Name	Rent Amount	Date Moved In
Adams, Carly	$300.00	11/2/93
Bush, Dan	$300.00	6/30/93
Larson, Michael	$375.00	4/1/93
Majors, Heath	$250.00	8/12/90
Philips, Mary	$275.00	6/15/93
Smith, Martha	$300.00	6/1/93
	$0.00	

Record: 1

YIKES!

You thought that a form displayed only one record at a time! Why did you think that? Did you believe everything you read in this book? Seriously, forms, such as the tabular form shown here, can display more than one record at a time, but the display is meant to be used much differently from that of a datasheet view. When lots of records have to be seen, edited, and entered, a datasheet view can't be beat for its clean, no-frills appearance. Nevertheless, forms are more professional looking and put end users (and computer novices) more at ease. Forms are designed to show fewer records than a datasheet (and forms like the single-column forms you designed in earlier chapters are designed to show only one record).

7. Close and save the form under the name Mid-Price and Qtly Renters, and return to the database window.

Chapter Wrap-Up

You are now a form wizard! You can add complex criteria selection to your forms so that the end user works with a nice-looking form that displays the data needed.

The AND (and its cousin BETWEEN) operator combines relational operators to produce range testing for data. You can test to see whether fields fall within a certain date range, letter range, name range, or numeric range. The OR operator enables you to select one of several different relations.

When you want to extend an AND and OR (or is it AND or OR? AND and/or OR??) relation across fields, Access knows that you want to do so by the way you specify the criteria for the two fields. If you place one field's criteria on the same row as another field's, an implied AND relation takes place between them. If you place one field's criteria on a different row from another field's, an implied OR relation takes place between them.

Diving In

- Use AND to test ranges of data.
- Use BETWEEN as a shortcut operator for AND.
- Use OR when one of several possible values needs to be tested.
- Specify AND and OR across fields (as opposed to a more focused relation inside the same field) by placing the criteria on the same or different rows across the query's fields.

Sunk

- Don't confuse a query with a table. A query is a subset of a table, and a table is the entire set of records. Nevertheless, you can treat dynasets (the resulting data from a query) just like a regular table of data and create forms (and reports, as you'll see in Part VI of this book) from the queries.

Part VI
Multiple Tables

How Do I Add More Tables?

Relate Them If You Can

● *Friendly Relatives*   212
● *One-to-One Table Relationships*   213
● *One-to-Many Table Relationships*   214
● *Many-to-Many Table Relationships*   216
● *Adding a Table*   217
● *Putting Data in the Table*   218

Are you getting tired of working with the same Tenant Data table? So is Laura Landlady. She needs to start keeping track of her property data so that she'll know a tenant's address when she mails the tenant a past-due letter (or a year-end discount for paying on time).

This chapter begins with a little discussion on relating database tables. Many (but not all) tables within the same database relate to each other. One field generally relates one table to another. After a little theory about table relationships (*theory*, in this sense, does not imply that table relationships are difficult), the middle of this chapter supplies data you must enter for a new table. After you've entered the data, you'll see how Access enables you to define the table relationships in the database. The next few chapters will use those relationships to pull data out of two tables at the same time.

Friendly Relatives

In database terminology, there are three primary ways to relate one table to another. Most of the theory behind relating data also applies to data stored in a filing cabinet. Chapter 1, "What's Access All About?" described keeping your financial records in a filing cabinet. Your checkbook file is different from your insurance file, yet the two are related in one sense: a check number in the checkbook file describes a transaction in the insurance file every time you pay an insurance bill.

The way to relate two tables is to put a common field in both.

The three ways that tables can relate are

- One-to-one

- One-to-many

- Many-to-many

When you are linking tables, the common field between them works most efficiently if that field is a primary key field, although Access does not require the common field to be a primary key field.

One-to-One Table Relationships

The one-to-one relationship is the least common. When database developers find themselves creating a one-to-one relationship, they often find that both tables should be combined into a single table with more fields rather than having two or more tables with fewer fields each.

A one-to-one relationship applies when one table contains records that all have a match, via the common field, to records in another table.

Access sets an upper limit of 255 fields per table. If you needed a table with more fields (*wow!*), you would have to break the table into two tables, with each record in the first table linking up with a record in the second table via a common field. Simulating one long table is perhaps the only advantage of a one-to-one relationship.

One-to-Many Table Relationships

The one-to-many relationship will be demonstrated in this chapter when you create a property table. You will create a property table with Property ID as its primary key field. In each of the Tenant Data table's records, there is a field named Property ID that will form the link between the two tables.

In our same Tenant data table, there are only two tenants listed who have lived in the same property. As Figure 19.1 shows, Terrie Johnson lived in property H2 at one time (she moved out on May 30, 1993), and Mary Philips lives there now. There is a one-to-many (or many-to-one, looking at the tables from the other direction) relationship with one property relating to two tenants. As Laura Landlady adds tenants over time, she will have other people moving out of and into properties, and her one-to-many relationships will grow. Thankfully, after she tells Access to maintain this relationship, Access will do all the work of relating the tables as she adds data in the future.

Consider this scenario: The tenant's data should remain separate from the property's data (such as address, price paid for the property, and so on). However, Laura might want to print a report showing each of her current tenants and their addresses rather than just a property ID code. Therefore, we'll create a query in the next chapter that grabs data from *both* tables rather than just one table. The query itself is what describes the relation between two tables in your database.

HMM...

Access does not magically know which field will be the link field when you want to join two tables. Just because two or more tables share the same field name doesn't mean they are related by that field. You must tell Access to relate the tables by a common field and specify which field that is. When Laura wants a Tenant ID, the query can then link up to the matching record in the Property table to find that tenant's address.

Figure 19.1.

Illustrating a one- (a property) to-many (two tenants) relationship.

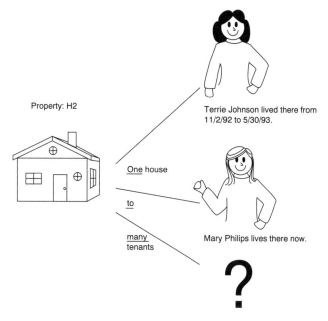

Property: H2

One house

to

many tenants

Terrie Johnson lived there from 11/2/92 to 5/30/93.

Mary Philips lives there now.

Someone else will live there someday.

YIKES!

Again, I keep coming back to the fact that although you might not be creating a database for rental properties, your database requirements, especially when you're first developing simple databases as a newcomer to Access, will be *exactly* like those that Laura faces. Your database might have a customer table that matches products bought, or inventory items that match several vendors which supply each of those items.

Many-to-Many Table Relationships

The many-to-many relationship occurs when several records in one table relate to several records in another. For example, Laura might keep track of several workers she hires from time to time. Each of those workers might work on more than one property.

Retail business databases often provide a perfect example of a many-to-many relationship: There are many customers who buy many products. More than one customer will buy more than one product, and the same kind of product might be bought by many different customers.

HMM... In theory, the Tenant Data table and the Property ID table could take on a many-to-many relationship over time. A tenant might live in two or more properties over time. Also, if a tenant really likes Laura, that tenant might move out of one property only to move into another of Laura's properties later.

Skip This, It's Technical

Master the one-to-many relationship first (as demonstrated in this book). You'll find that it's the most useful of the three kinds of table relationships. The only way to create a many-to-many relationship in Access is to create a third table that contains all the common fields of the other two tables. This third table will go between the other two. You'll have to specify a many-to-one relationship from the first table to the new table, then create a one-to-many relationship from the middle table to the last table. Access does not directly support many-to-many relationships.

Adding a Table

Adding another table to your database is almost tedium at this point. You are so used to selecting New from the database window for queries and forms that doing the same thing for a new table is simple. Nevertheless, the next few chapters must have data to work with, so follow these steps to create a Property Data table:

1. Open the RENTALS database if it is not already open. Click the Table button, and select New.

2. Create the table from the following field names, data types, widths, and descriptions. (Remember that you specify the width in the Field Properties area in the lower pane of the window.)

Field Name	Data Type	Width	Description
Property ID	Text	3	ID of property
Address	Text	25	Address of property
City	Text	10	City name
State	Text	2	State name
Zip	Text	10	ZIP code
Date Bought	Date		Date of purchase
Price Paid	Currency		Price of property
Notes	Memo		Description and misc.

PSST!
All of Laura's properties are in Oklahoma. Therefore, move the row selector to the State field, and click the Default Value box. Type OK. You've now learned about another property. A default value will appear automatically when you enter data in a datasheet or form view. Of course, the user can always replace the default value with something else while entering the record's data.

YIKES!

Even though the property's table and the tenant's table both have Notes fields, only the Property ID field is the common field that will relate the two fields. The next chapter will relate the two tables using a query. The reason you have to tell Access specifically which tables to relate is that not all common fields in all tables should form a relationship, and the Notes field is a good example of why.

3. Move the row selector so that it points to the Property ID field, and select Edit Set Primary Key.

HMM...

When you specify the field as a primary key, you'll notice that Access fills in the last of this field's property box with YES (No Duplicates), meaning that no two properties can have the same ID. The "one side" of a one-to-many relationship should always specify the common field as the primary key field.

4. Save the table's format by closing the window. Name the table Property Data when prompted by Access.

Putting Data in the Table

Now for some typing. There aren't many properties, so please take the time to enter these data values into the new table after selecting Open from the database window.

Field Name	Data

Record 1

Property ID	H1
Address	220 N. Illinois
City	Hilltown
State	OK
Zip	74133
Date Bought	10/4/93
Price Paid	57643.00
Notes	3-BR house on corner of Illinois and Boston

Record 2

Property ID	A1a
Address	919 S. "C" Street, #1
City	Hilltown
State	OK
Zip	74154
Date Bought	7/7/90
Price Paid	313454.00
Notes	4-plex townhouse apartment building, Unit #1

Record 3

Property ID	A1b
Address	919 S. "C" Street, #2
City	Hilltown
State	OK
Zip	74154
Date Bought	7/7/90
Price Paid	313454.00
Notes	4-plex townhouse apartment building, Unit #2

continues

Field Name	*Data*

Record 4

Property ID	A1c
Address	919 S. "C" Street, #3
City	Hilltown
State	OK
Zip	74154
Date Bought	7/7/90
Price Paid	313454.00
Notes	4-plex townhouse apartment building, Unit #3

Record 5

Property ID	A1d
Address	919 S. "C" Street, #4
City	Hilltown
State	OK
Zip	74154
Date Bought	7/7/90
Price Paid	313454.00
Notes	4-plex townhouse apartment building, Unit #4

Record 6

Property ID	H2
Address	304 West Sycamore
City	Port City
State	OK
Zip	74389
Date Bought	9/6/92
Price Paid	62323.00
Notes	2-BR house with siding and 2-car garage

Record 7

Property ID	H3
Address	5212 East Tenth
City	Sycamore
State	OK

Field Name	Data
Zip	74351
Date Bought	8/19/93
Price Paid	94384.00
Notes	3-BR house (zoned for commercial use)

Record 8

Property ID	H4
Address	7560 East 26th Place
City	Tulsa
State	OK
Zip	74129
Date Bought	3/22/93
Price Paid	59434.00
Notes	3-BR house

Record 9

Property ID	D1
Address	5223 South Yardley
City	Tulsa
State	OK
Zip	74152
Date Bought	1/30/93
Price Paid	102173.00
Notes	Duplex, Unit #1

Record 10

Property ID	D2
Address	5227 South Yardley
City	Tulsa
State	OK
Zip	74152
Date Bought	1/30/93
Price Paid	102173.00
Notes	Duplex, Unit #2

Laura's four-plex apartment buildings have similar Property IDs, each distinguished by a letter that indicates which unit is being described.

YIKES!

You might notice from the dates that you are not entering the properties in the order in which they were bought. The order in which you enter data has no bearing on how you see that data later with queries and reports.

Close the table and get ready to link the Property Data table to the Tenant Data table in the next chapter.

Chapter Wrap-Up

The purpose of this chapter was to teach you the three methods of relating database tables: one-to-one, one-to-many, and many-to-many. Most often, you'll need a one-to-many relationship. Before relating a table to the Tenant Data table in the next chapter, you had to take the time to enter a new table in this chapter. The last part of this chapter was spent describing the new table and data that represent Laura Landlady's rental properties. Now that you've got two tables in the database, you're ready to earn your advanced Access degree by viewing data in both tables at once.

Diving In

- Learn the differences between the three table-relationship methods.

- As you create a database and add tables to the database, keep in mind that related tables must contain a common field.

Sunk

- Don't forget to make the "one side" table of the one-to-many relationship contain a primary key field that is the common field between that table and the "many side" table.

- Despite the tediousness of typing data, don't forget any of the values in the Property Data table. Future chapters rely on having this data.

How Can I See Two Tables?

Use a Multiple-Table Query

- The Makeup of a Multiple-Table Query   227
- Creating the Query   228
- Fixing a Problem   231
- Turning a Dynaset into a Table   233

Now that you've added a second table to the database, you'll want to look at the data. Of course, looking at the data from within the table *by itself* is easy. The real world, however, demands more than single-table database views. For example, Laura needs to be able to print listings of her tenants' names and their addresses for a phone and address list. The problem is that there is not a table that contains both the tenant names and phone numbers and the addresses. The Tenant Data table contains the tenant names and phone numbers, and the Property Data table contains the property addresses. As usual, Access rushes to the rescue by enabling you to create queries that retrieve data from two or more tables at once.

 HMM...   Remember that a query produces a dynaset that you can treat as if the dynaset were a table in your database. A dynaset is really *not* a stand-alone table, but you can send the contents of a dynaset to a form or report just as if you were sending a table to be viewed with the form or report.

PSST!   There are ways to store a dynaset as a new table in case you want to give another Access user a subset of your data. The last part of this chapter explains how to create a new table from a query.

Creating a multiple-table query is fairly straightforward, but not necessarily intuitive. After you see the steps in creating a multiple-table query from within the query definition window, you'll have no trouble creating your own multiple-table queries. In this chapter you'll create a multiple-table query, and in the next chapter you'll learn how to look at that query's result from within forms.

The Makeup of a Multiple-Table Query

Creating a multiple-table query requires that you *join* the two tables. Access uses a common field to join the records properly. You can join more than one table at once, as long as every table contains some field in common with at least one of the other tables.

In the previous queries, you specified only one table and selected fields from that table that you wanted to appear in the resulting dynaset. To create a query from two tables, you'll have to first tell Access the name of the two tables in the query and then select fields from both tables.

Skip This, It's Technical

By specifying a common field that joins the two tables, you will ensure that the tables stay synchronized. If you did not join the two tables, Access would display the Tenant Data's first tenant name and the Property Data's first address. The next record that appears in the dynaset will be the second records from the two tables. The Tenant Data table, however, is *not* listed in the same order as the Property Data table. By joining the tables with a common field, you'll ensure that *each* tenant's name from the Tenant Data table correctly matches with the correct address in the Property Data table.

In review, you'll follow these three steps to create a multiple-table query:

1. Create a new query, and specify all the tables that will help build the resulting dynaset.

2. Join the tables with their common field (or fields, if applicable).

3. Select the fields from each table that you want to appear in the resulting dynaset, including sorting and selecting information if you need it.

Creating the Query

The following steps create a multiple-table query for Laura Landlady:

1. Open the Rentals database if it is not already open.

2. Click the Query button, and select New. Access displays the Add Table dialog box. Remember that a query might get its data from tables, queries, or both.

3. Highlight the Property Data table, and select Add. You'll see the Property Data field-selection box appear in the upper pane of the query definition window.

4. Highlight the Tenant Data table, and select Add. As with the previous table, you'll see the Tenant Data's field-selection box appear next to the Property Data's field-selection box on-screen.

5. Select Close to close the Add Table dialog box and display the query's definition window.

PSST! Now would be a good time to move the Tenant Data field-selection box to the right a little (add about an inch between the boxes) by dragging the box's title bar to the right with the mouse. Widen the two boxes by dragging each of their right edges to the right so that their full field names come into view.

6. Now it's time to join the tables. You can mess with the menus to connect the tables, but there is a much easier way. Click and hold the mouse button over the Property ID field in the Property Data box, and drag the field name to the second table until it rests over the Property ID field in the second table. Release the mouse. Access takes care of the rest by drawing a line from the first table to the second, as shown in Figure 20.1.

Figure 20.1.

Access graphic-ally shows you the join between the tables.

The join line

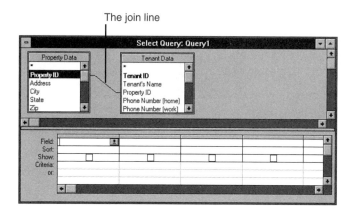

7. Now that you've joined the tables by a common field, the last job is to select those fields from both tables that you want to see. Drag the Tenant's Name from the Tenant Data field table to the first Field box in the lower pane. Click the Sort box under Tenant's Name, and select Ascending to sort the names alphabetically. The resulting query will be displayed in tenant-name order.

8. Finish the query by dragging the Phone Number (home) field (from the Tenant Data table) to the second Field column, then the Address, City, State, and Zip fields (from the Property Data field box) down to the lower pane's Field boxes. Be sure that all the Show boxes remain checked because you want all these fields to appear in the resulting query. Your screen will look like the one in Figure 20.2.

Figure 20.2.

After selecting all the fields for the query.

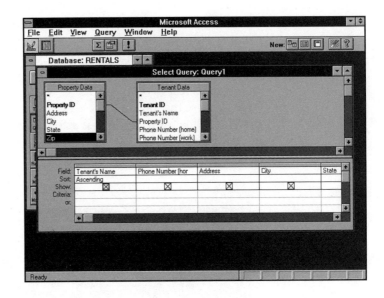

YIKES!

Even though the Property Data table appears to the left of the Tenant Data table, we selected fields from the Tenant Data table to appear first in the query. The order in which you selected the tables has no bearing on the order of the resulting query's fields.

9. Save the query under the name Phone Book.

10. Click the datasheet view tool (the second tool from the left on the toolbar), and you'll see the resulting phone book dynaset. You might want to resize the dynaset to full screen and widen some of the columns (such as the Address column) so that their data fits nicely within the view.

Fixing a Problem

If you look closely at the dynaset created from the Phone Book query, you'll spot a problem. Both Terrie Johnson and Mary Philips seem to live in the same house! What's the problem?

The Tenant Data table contains all current tenants as well as previous tenants. Terrie Johnson has moved out, but her record still appears (as it is supposed to) in the Tenant Data table so that Laura Landlady can keep track of tenant history. However, if Laura wants a listing of just the current tenants' phone numbers and addresses, she certainly does not want former tenants appearing in her phone list.

Therefore, you'll have to change the way the Phone Book query selects records by following these steps:

1. Click the design tool (the far-left tool on the toolbar) to return to the query definition window.

2. Scroll the lower pane until a blank column (the one to the right of Zip) comes into view.

3. Drag the Date Moved Out field from the Tenant Data table to the new Field box in the lower pane.

4. Deselect the Show button so that the Date Moved Out field does not appear in the resulting query but is still used to select the query's records.

5. Select the Date Moved Out column's Criteria box, and type this into the box:

   ```
   =Null
   ```

YIKES!

Two things happen when you press Enter. Access changes the criteria box to read `Is Null`, and you wonder what this `Null` business is all about! `Null` is a keyword in Access which means that nothing exists in the field. Nothing does exist in any of the *current* tenants' Date Moved Out fields (because they haven't moved out), but there will always be a value in the date Moved Out field for former tenants. By specifying `=Null` (you could have typed `Is Null`), you are telling the query to select only those records that have no value yet for the Date Moved Out field.

6. Select the datasheet view tool again to view the resulting query. Your screen should look something like the one in Figure 20.3 (after widening the Address column) with the correct phone listing for current tenants only.

Figure 20.3.

Looking at current tenants only.

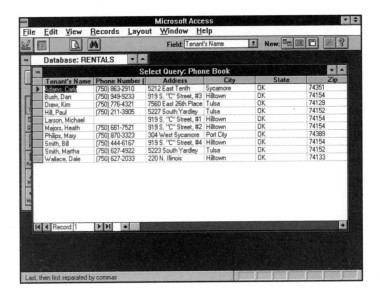

7.   Close the datasheet view and save the query.

Turning a Dynaset into a Table

If you want a query's result to be stored in a table (in effect, creating a subset table from one or more other tables), Access enables you to create such a *make-table* query.

YIKES!

A make-table query does not create a new dynaset, but a completely new and separate table. A dynaset contains active data; if the underlying table's data changes, so does a dynaset's. However, a make-table query produces a separate and distinct table from the original table. Therefore, if the original table's data changes, the table produced with an earlier make-table query will not change.

The following steps use the Phone Book multiple-table query to generate a new table in case Laura wants to copy her current tenants' name and address records onto her secretary's computer for mailing purposes.

1.   Select the query Phone Book, and click the Design button to open the query in its design view.

2.   From the pull-down menu, select Query Make Table..., and Access displays the Query Properties dialog box shown in Figure 20.4.

Figure 20.4.

Getting ready to turn the query into a table.

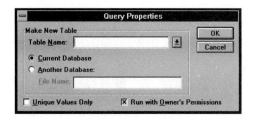

Access enables you to save the query to a table in a different database (you would have to supply the other database name in the File Name box), but for this example, leave Current Database selected. You could also save only those records that are unique, but as long as you've designated a primary key field, every record will be unique. The Run with Owner's Permission provides network security control if it's needed. Most of the time, you'll simply want to save the resulting query in a table in the current database, and the Query Properties window default values take care of that.

3. Type the name `Phone Book Data`, and press Enter (or click OK).

4. You now have to *run* the query. Running a query is slightly different from looking at the results of a regular query. A make-table query is known as an *action query.* All action queries must be run, not just opened. There are two ways to run the query: select Query Run from the menus, or click the Run tool, which is the exclamation point.

    After a brief pause, Access tells you how many records will be copied to the new table and asks you to OK the copy with the dialog box shown in Figure 20.5. Select OK and Access makes the table.

5. Close the query window, save the change, and look at the difference in the database window. Access lets you know that the query is now an action query by prefacing its name with an exclamation point (to remind you that you have to run the query).

6. Click the Table button, and you'll see the new table named Phone Book Data that was created from the make-table query.

Figure 20.5.

OK'ing the make-table query.

PSST! The Phone Book query is now an action query, and it cannot be used as a regular dynaset-creating query any longer. If you want both a dynaset Phone Book query and a make-table query, you'll first have to copy the query (by selecting the query in the database window, then choosing Edit Copy and Edit Paste to copy the query) to a new query name. Then you'll need to change the query's action to a *select-only* (the dynaset-creating kind) query by selecting Query Select from the menu.

Chapter Wrap-Up

Working with individual tables is fine for simple database work, but the true power is unleashed when you are able to join two or more tables together, by a common field, and retrieve data from both at the same time. This chapter taught you about multiple-table queries. To create a multiple-table query, you simply have to drag the common field from one table to another to create the join. Access draws a line between the two tables, thus visually showing you how the tables relate. Pulling data from the joined tables is then a snap, and Access makes the multiple-table query almost as easy as a single-table query.

Although most queries produce dynasets (which look and kind of act like tables but are not actually separate tables), you can turn a query's result into a table by making the query a make-table query. When you run a make-table query, Access copies the queried data out of the underlying table (or tables) into a brand new table of data.

Diving In

- Generate a multiple-table query whenever you need data from two or more tables at once.

- A query must be a make-table query if you want to produce a stand-alone table from the query. A make-table is known as an action query that you must run from the menu or by clicking the Run tool.

Sunk

- Don't generate a multiple-table query unless you have joined the tables by a common field. Without the join, the data from the tables will not be in synch, and the data from one will not match the data pulled from the other.

Will a Form Work with Two Tables?

Use a Subform: A Form Within a Form

- *Relate the Tables First*   238
- *Creating a Subform*   240

Creating a multiple-table form can be as easy as creating a single-table form. Instead of specifying a single table when creating the form (with FormWizards), you specify the multiple-table query. Creating a form using a multiple-table query is rather elementary at this point: Create a new form, and with FormWizards specify the multiple-table form for the form's data source.

How about trying the advanced task of displaying a form from one table inside the form of another table? With just a little effort, you can create a form that contains a *subform*. A subform is a form inside another form (the outside form is the *main* form). If you want to give the user a chance to look up related data from one table while adding or viewing data in another table, a subform is the way to do it.

Relate the Tables First

Fun Fact

An advantage of explicitly relating the tables rather than the database automatically relating them when it sees fields with the same names is that you can relate tables with fields that aren't named the same.

Tables aren't automatically related just because both contain a field with the same name. A multiple-table query links two tables by a common field just for the life of the query's operation. You can, however, create a permanent table relationship between two tables. After you create that relationship, you can use FormWizards to create a form-subform relationship.

Remember the description of a one-to-many relationship? (Chapter 19, "How Do I Add More Tables?" explained different relationship possibilities.) With only two tables, Laura doesn't have a lot of choice, but whether you are working with 2 or 20 tables, relating tables is just as easy. In Laura Landlady's case, there is a one-to-many relationship between the Property Data table and the Tenant Data table. Recall that there can be more than one tenant for a single property because former tenants are being saved in the table.

By specifying a one-to-many relationship with the following steps, you not only inform Access of the relationship, but you can then create a form-subform as well.

Create the Property Data table/Tenant Data table relationship by following these steps:

1. Click the Table button in the database window, and highlight the Property Data table.

2. Select Edit Relationships... to display the Relationships window shown in Figure 21.1.

Figure 21.1.

Getting ready to create a table relationship.

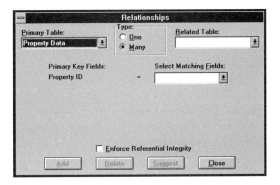

Access fills in the Primary Table box with the Property Data table for you (the *one* in the one-to-many relationship). The Many option is already clicked (indicating that the next table you choose will be on the *many* side).

3. Select the Tenant Data table in the Related Table box.

4. Press Alt+S to request that Access suggest the common linking field. Access finds the common field (Property ID) and inserts it in the Select Matching Fields box. (You could have typed the name or selected it from the pull-down list.)

5. Click the Add button and close the Relationships window. You've now linked the table.

PSST!   After you set up a table relationship, if you ever create a query using both of the tables, Access will automatically join those tables with the join line (which you had to create manually in the preceding chapter).

Creating a Subform

FormWizards is such a help for creating powerful forms! You'll see with your own eyes, but you won't even believe it. (OK, maybe this is too big of a build-up, but if you ever try to create a subform with other database products, you'll appreciate Access's simplicity and power.)

Laura does not yet have a property form for the Property Data table. When Laura looks at a property, she wants to know who is living in that property, as well as a history of who has lived there in the past. This might seem like quite a chore, but not for Access. Follow these steps to make the powerful Property form with an embedded Tenant subform:

1. Click the Forms button in the database window, and click the New button.

2. Select the Property Data table in the Select a Table/Query box, and click the FormWizards button to start FormWizards.

3. Look at the screen, and you'll instantly know what to do to create the form and subform. Select the Main/Subform item from the group of form designs. Access displays the dialog box shown in Figure 21.2.

Figure 21.2.

*You must tell
Access which
table will be
embedded.*

 HMM...

The two Tenant forms you created earlier contained
no subforms, so you did not see the dialog box shown
in Figure 21.2 then.

4. Select the Tenant Data table, and click the Next> button.

5. FormWizards returns to a familiar screen wanting to know
    which of the Property Data table fields you want on the form.
    Select all the fields by clicking the >> button, and then click
    the Next> button.

6. Access needs to know which fields you want to see on the
    subform. The primary focus of this form will be property data,
    but Laura wants to see each property's tenant names as well.
    A phone number might be nice also. Therefore, move the
    Tenant's Name and Phone Number (home) fields to the
    Fields on subform scrolling list so that your screen looks like
    the one in Figure 21.3.

7. Select the Standard form look, type `Property Information` for
    the form's title, and click the Open button. Access surprises
    you with a dialog box that looks like an error message
    (Figure 21.4), but everything is fine.

Figure 21.3.

After selecting the subform fields.

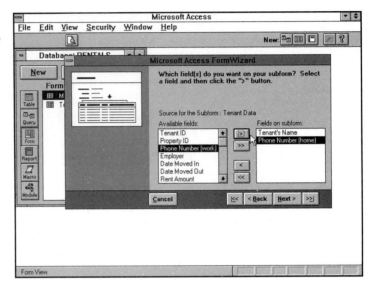

Figure 21.4.

Access requires that you save the subform.

Before FormWizards can finish the Property form (the main form), you must save the subform you created along the way. Save the form under the name Property's Tenant Subform.

After a brief pause, Access displays the first property's record, and you'll find the tenant who lives in that property listed in the subform at the bottom of the form.

PSST!

Resize the form (by double-clicking the main form's title bar) to full-screen so that you can see the entire form and subform, as shown in Figure 21.5.

Figure 21.5.

*Displaying the
first property
record and that
property's tenant.*

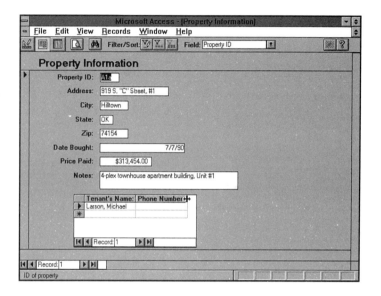

> ## YIKES!
>
> It is just a coincidence that Michael Larsen, who lives in
> the first property, doesn't have a phone number. Press
> Page Down to see the next few records, and you'll see phone
> numbers listed.

You can scroll both of the forms (the main form and the subform)
individually because they each contain their own set of record-
selection buttons. Scroll to the property on West Sycamore to see
two tenants, the current one and the one who lived there previously.
(Perhaps Laura should consider adding the Date Moved Out field to
the subform so that she'll know exactly who lives in the property
and can also see a history of the property's occupancy dates. If she
wants to do so, she can rerun FormWizards or add the field by hand
from the design view.)

HMM...   You cannot resize or move the subform because it is attached to the main form and anchored in the location decided on by FormWizards. However, you can go into design view and manually select and move the subform if you want to.

Notice that as you scroll through the properties, the subform's data updates to reflect each property's tenant. Access could not have achieved this linking of forms if the tables had not been related by a common field.

Chapter Wrap-Up

In this chapter, you created a table relationship by telling Access how the Property Data and the Tenant Data tables related. Tables relate by sharing a common field. After the tables are related, you can create some powerful form and subform combinations by answering a few FormWizards questions.

This book has so far dedicated itself to viewing data inside the datasheet and form views, but the screen is not the only place you'll want to see your data. Starting in the next chapter, you'll learn how to create printed reports.

Diving In

- Explicitly create a relationship between two tables to ease multiple-table query creation and, more important, to allow for a form/subform relationship.

- Make minor sizing modifications to your forms from the design view. All the form modifications described in Chapter 15, "How Do I Improve My Form's Appearance?" work for both the main form and its subform.

Sunk

- Don't attempt to create a subform inside a form if the under-lying tables aren't properly related. Access will attempt to relate the tables in the two forms as best it can, but Access guesses badly.

- Don't display too many fields in a subform. Subforms are great for displaying two to four fields of data that relate to the main form's record.

Part VII
Advanced Reporting

How Do I Create Reports?

ReportWizards Makes Report-Writing Easy

- *Be a Wizard with ReportWizards* 250
- *Adding Some Grouping* 254

With many databases, creating simple reports is easy; creating good-looking, meaningful, and appealing reports is agonizing at best. As usual, Access bucks the trend by providing ReportWizards, a step-by-step guide that walks you through the creation of professional reports by asking you a few simple questions along the way.

HMM... Way back in Chapter 13, "Can I Print Data?" you saw how to print datasheet and form view data listings, but a *report* is generally considered to be more professional-looking and customized with optional headings and footings.

Access can also provide a screen preview of the printed report before sending the report to the printer. Again, Access is trying to save you time. Looking at a report on-screen is faster than printing it. Preview your report on-screen and *then* decide whether you want to print the report or change it before sending the report to paper.

Be a Wizard with ReportWizards

As with forms, you don't have to use AccessWizards to create a report—but it sure helps! You can control the placement of any report element (titles, data, totals, and so forth), but because Access comes equipped with many common (and appealing) styles, you probably will rarely have to go into the design view of a report to modify what gets printed.

The following steps create a report that displays the tenant names, property IDs, and rental amounts of each tenant. We'll print each of the report's records in rent amount order, from low to high. A total of the rents will be printed at the bottom of the report. All this is done through the help of ReportWizards.

1. Click the Report button in the database window, and then select New.

2. Scroll the Select a Table/Query until you can select Tenant Data.

3. Click the ReportWizards button, and you'll see the report selection window shown in Figure 22.1.

Figure 22.1.

Selecting a report type.

4. Choose Groups/Totals and click OK.

5. You rarely want every one of a table's fields to print on a report because the report records would be too long. There-fore, one at a time as you did when creating a form, select a field—begin with Tenant ID—and press the > key. In the same way, select Tenant's Name, Property ID, and Rent Amount so that they appear in the Field order on report scrolling list, and click Next>.

Skip This, It's Technical

If you indicate that you want every field to appear on a report (by clicking the >> button), all the table's (or query's) fields will appear on the final printed report. Of course, there are usually more fields than will fit on a single page. Access prints as many fields as possible on the first page, then continues the fields onto the next printed page (and this continues if needed until all the fields are printed). You can then tape the pages next to each other to make a wide, oversized report.

6. Access wants to know how you want the report grouped. If your data were to consist of values that could be grouped, such as sales by district or total by product (just about any time you want a *something by something*), you could group the report by a certain field. Generally, you would group your data if it had repeating values in a field. None of the fields in this report consists of repeating groups of any kind, so select Next>.

7. Sort the report by the Rent Amount field by sending the Rent Amount field to the Sort order of records in groups box. This ensures that the report prints in Rent Amount order.

8. Select the Executive report. Access wants you to add a report title to the top of the report, so type `Total Tenant Rental Report`

YIKES!

Don't confuse a report *title* with the *name* of a report. The title appears at the top of the report; the report name is the name you select when you want to print the report.

9. Select the Print Preview button, and wait a few moments. Access displays a screen preview of your report like the one shown in Figure 22.2. Your report looks great!

10. Press the Page Down key to look at the bottom half of the report. You'll see that the Rent Amount's total automatically appears at the bottom of the report. Access totals all numeric fields at the bottom of the report. If your data were such that you could print a grouped report, Access would subtotal each group as well.

Figure 22.2.

Previewing the report.

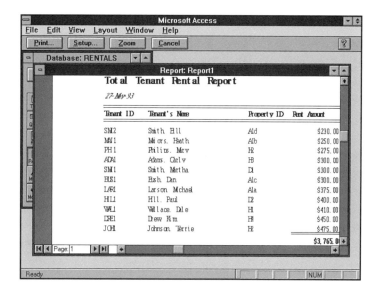

PSST! Click the mouse button to make Access show you a thumbnail sketch of the full report, as shown in Figure 22.3. With only a little data, the report looks somewhat out of balance, but most data takes more than a single page and fills the report page better. Anyway, the report looks pretty good, even with only 11 records!

HMM... If you like what you see in the preview, click the Print... button to print the report.

11. Save the report under the name Rent Total Report. If you change the table's data, then print the report again, you'll see that Access reports with the latest changes.

Figure 22.3.

Looking at a bird's-eye view of the report.

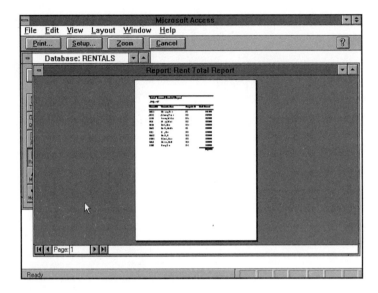

Adding Some Grouping

The tenant report that you created in the preceding section does not lend itself to a true grouping method. For instance, Laura Landlady does not need a listing of each tenant by state because every tenant lives in the same state. Access does provide a useful reporting feature for data that you want to see grouped together by ranges of values. A picture is worth a thousand words, so follow these steps to create a report that breaks the tenants into groups based on their rent-amount ranges:

1. Click the Report button in the database window, and then select New.

2. Scroll the Select a Table/Query until you can select Tenant Data.

3. Click the ReportWizards button to display the report selection window.

4. Select Groups/Totals because you're creating a report (rather, ReportWizards is creating it, and you're helping).

5. As before, select the following fields to display in the report:

   Tenant ID   Tenant's Name   Property ID   Rent Amount

   Select the Rent Amount field by clicking, then go to the next screen with Next>. Access displays the window shown in Figure 22.4 that specifies the field you want to be used for the grouping.

Figure 22.4.

Telling Access how to group the report.

6. You'll see the grouping window shown in Figure 22.5, which appears a little strange at first.

Figure 22.5.

Specifying how you want the data grouped.

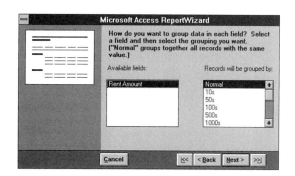

Skip This, It's Technical

If you were grouping by a text field rather than the numeric Rent Amount field, Access would have displayed a different window from the one shown in Figure 22.5. When you group by a numeric field, Access offers you a choice of how you want the numeric data grouped. If lots of Laura's Rent Amounts were the same—for instance, if she had three divisions of properties, $400, $500, and $600—she would want a Normal grouping so that every $400 property was grouped (and subtotaled), every $500 property was grouped, and every $600 property was grouped. However, because most of the Rent Amount values are different from each other, selecting the 50s grouping value prints the tenant records grouped by every $50. (All the tenants who pay from $300 to $350 will print together, those who pay from $350 to $400 will print together, and so on.) If you were grouping by a text field, Access would ask whether you wanted to group by the first character in the field, the first two characters, and so on.

7.   Select the 50s option and press Next>. We'll print the tenants in Tenant ID order *within each group,* so select Tenant ID and then the Executive style.

8.   Type `Tenant Rent Group Report` for the title and select Print Preview. Wait a moment while Access generates the report. After looking at the report on-screen, you can print it by selecting the Print... button in the upper-left corner of the screen. The final printed report looks good, doesn't it?

HMM...   The report would look better if there were more data. The rental property database in this book has been kept small because you shouldn't be spending all your time entering data when you could be seeing more

features of Access. I hope that you'll appreciate the fact that less space is devoted to raw data entry and more is devoted to the features. The rental property database contains all the fundamental elements of any database, so as you create your own, you'll be able to see how to edit and print your own data by following the example of this book's database.

Chapter Wrap-Up

This chapter's goal was to teach you some of the features of the ReportWizards report-creation system in Access. Producing a report is extremely easy. You saw that Access will total numeric fields or group by fields, depending on your needs.

Creating a report with ReportWizards is just as easy as creating a form with FormWizards. Their similarity makes it easier to remember each system. Microsoft, the designer of Access, could have chosen to offer completely different systems for creating forms and reports, as a lot of competing products do, but then there would be more to learn and another set of barriers to break before you could become an Access pro.

After you've created a report with ReportWizards, you can change the report using the Design button on the database window. Most of the time, however, you'll like what ReportWizards produces. Try some of the different reporting options in ReportWizards to see what is possible.

Diving In

- Use ReportWizards to help you create reports.

- If you want more than simple totals at the bottom of your report, consider grouping your printed data. Grouping is especially helpful when you have a need to report data *by* some other data, such as producing a report of sales by division. (Access would subtotal each division's numeric fields, then display a grand total at the bottom.)

Sunk

- Don't group with the Normal option if your grouped field contains lots of values that are different from each other.

- Don't be afraid to adjust the grouping method until you find the right one for your data. If you first group by 50s or 100s and then realize that the groups are too small, try grouping by 500s or 1000s. Your data and your application's needs determine what you need in the long run.

How Do I Print Mailing Labels?

Design and Print the Label

- *What Do You Want?*   260
- *Let's Play Post Office*   261

We generally don't consider the fact that mailing labels, checks, and invoices are reports, but they are. Any time information is produced on paper, it's a report as far as the computer is concerned. Your job consists of telling the computer what the report will look like and then finding the right paper for your printer that fits the report, such as blank printer checks or mailing labels.

This chapter shows you how to produce mailing labels from your data. As usual, Access does most of the work for you with ReportWizards, but producing labels might not be as straight-forward as you first think.

YIKES!

To produce mailing labels, you only have to go to the office supply shop and buy some labels, and you're off and printing, right? Almost right. It might surprise you to learn that Access supports around *70* different mailing label styles! The hardest thing about producing mailing labels is deciding on which ones you want to use.

What Do You Want?

Fun Fact

Access can even save you money! Tell Access to print the labels in ZIP code order so that you can take advantage of bulk-rate mailings.

When you think of printed labels, you often think of mailing labels with name and address information. The title of this chapter is slightly misleading, however, because labels don't have to be mailing labels (although the ones generated in this chapter happen to be). There are inventory labels, name tag labels, price tag labels, sale discount labels, and many more kinds of labels. Access does not automatically produce a mailing label when you request a label, because mailings are just part of the things labels help you do.

When you want a label with ReportWizards, you have to tell Access exactly what kind of information (from a table or query's list of fields) you want on the label. If you want extra spaces between the label's data, tell Access you want the space. If you want commas, exclamation points, extra text (such as a message above a customer's mailing label that reads *Sale Ends Saturday!*), you tell Access and Access obeys your orders.

PSST!   As you'll soon see, Access enables you to describe the label's data with a calculator-style on-screen keypad that is fun to use.

Let's Play Post Office

Laura realizes that her rental empire is small now but is growing steadily. When she gets a few hundred more properties (she is very ambitious), she'll need to send her tenants routine mailings with mailing labels instead of writing on the envelopes by hand.

The Tenant Data does not contain the perfect table setup for a tenant mailing list system because the tenant's address information is not stored in the table (address data is in the Property Data table). Earlier in the book (Chapter 20, "How Can I See Two Tables?"), you created the Phone Book Data table from a query that selected the tenants' names from the Tenant Data table and the address fields from the Property Data table. Therefore, the mailing list created here will use the Phone Book Data table to gather the fields from both tables into one.

The following steps look lengthy, but most of a mailing label design is just like any other report's design, with one exception: the label's data can look *any* way you want it to. Access provides perhaps more by-the-hand guidance during the creation of a mailing label than you'll find in any other database program. At the same time it gives you extensive freedom.

Start Access and open the RENTALS database if it is not already open. Follow these steps to generate mailing labels that a professional print shop would envy (and use):

1. At the database window, click the Report button, and select New.

2. Select the Phone Book Data table, and select ReportWizards to start the report generation.

3. Select the Mailing Label style. As described earlier, a label does not have to contain mailing information. Access is a little too specific with the name *Mailing Label,* but we'll forgive Access this time.

   When you click OK, you'll see the famous (famous now that it appears in this book!) label-creation window shown in Figure 23.1. Study the figure and see whether you can figure out what to do next.

Figure 23.1.

Getting ready to design a label.

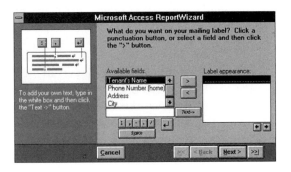

The side-by-side windows are now familiar to you. Access wants you to select which fields (by moving them to the right window) from the query that you want in the label. As you can see, Access does not assume that you want name and

address information printed (although a lot of times you will). You can send any field over to the right window by highlighting the field and clicking the > button.

YIKES!

Be careful! Although this set of windows looks like the same set you've seen by using FormWizards and the other ReportWizards option, there is a subtle difference. You aren't just telling Access *which* fields you want printed, but you're telling Access exactly where to place those fields as well.

PSST!   Think of this screen's right window as being the look of the label you are creating as well as the contents. If you want two fields to appear side-by-side, you will have to tell ReportWizards that is what you want.

4. Select the Tenant's Name field, and click > to send it to the right window. Now for the kicker: highlight the Address field, and click > to send it over—and *look where it landed!* Instead of appearing on the line beneath the name, the address appeared next to the name. Remember that you're designing the look of the label as well as the fields that will go on it.

   You won't want the address appearing right next to the name, so deselect the Address (a fancy term for putting it back on the left) by clicking the < button.

5. Instead of selecting a field, look at the list of buttons below the field list. You'll see a semicolon, a comma, and a hyphen, along with some other keys. To the far right is the symbol that appears on your keyboard's Enter key. You would click the Enter key button first if you wanted the next field to

appear below the previous one, just as you press Enter in a word processor to move the cursor to the next line. Therefore, click the Enter symbol, and you'll see that the highlight moves to the next line in the mailing label (Figure 23.2.). The second line of the label is awaiting your instruction.

Figure 23.2.

Clicking Enter to move to the next line on the label.

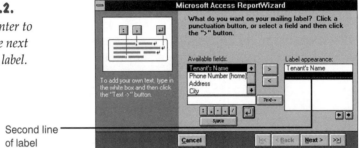

Second line of label

6. Click the Address field, and it will appear where it should in the right window. Click the Enter key again to move down to the third label line.

7. Move the City field to the label, but instead of clicking the Enter symbol, click the comma. After all, don't most people put a comma between the city and state? You can too. The data (neither the City field nor the State field) does not contain a comma, so you must instruct ReportWizards to insert one for you.

HMM... The post office doesn't like punctuation of any kind on a mailing label, but people usually put the comma between the city and state anyway. If you want to stick to the rules (and you should, but the comma is illustrative here), click the Space key rather than the Enter symbol to add a space between the city and state.

After the comma, click Space to put one space before the State. Access displays a blank as a dot. With a dot showing rather than a space, you'll be able to count how many spaces you've added if you ever need to.

Move the State field over, and then click the Space twice. Finally, move the Zip field over, and your window will look like the one in Figure 23.3.

Figure 23.3.

*After designing
the label.*

Label will look
like this

PSST! You can even add extra text on the label by typing text in the box to the left of the Text-> button and then clicking Text->.

8. Click Next> to move to the next screen. Select the Zip field to sort, and *then* select the Tenant's Name field to sort next. In previous report and form design, you specified only a single field for the sort, but there might be lots of tenants who live in the same ZIP code. By specifying a second field to sort by (called a *secondary sort key* by those in the industry who make up big words), Access sorts every tenant within each ZIP code alphabetically.

9. Click the Next> button, and you'll have another new window (Figure 23.4) to study.

Find the type of label you want to print to. For this example, try picking the Avery label 4144 (with three labels across each page), and press Next>.

Figure 23.4.

What kind of label are you printing to?

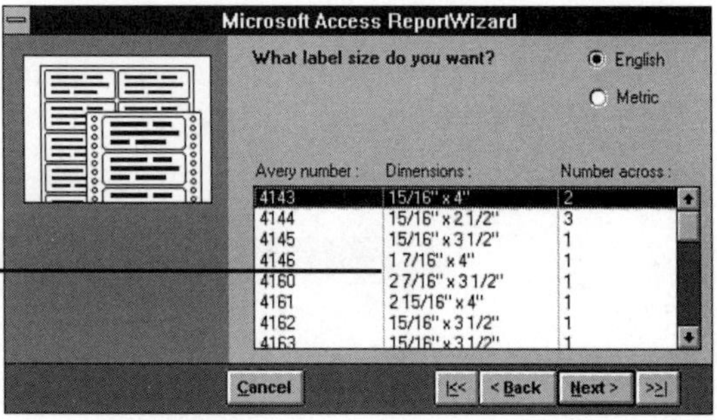

Select your label's dimensions from this list

Skip This, It's Technical

The label industry has many kinds of labels in many different sizes. There are labels with only one label per page (on small tear-apart pages), two-across labels with a column of the two labels next to each other on a page, and three-across labels. Each comes in all shapes and sizes. The label industry has different schemes for keeping track of the types of labels available. One of the most common numbering systems is the Avery label system because Avery sells more labels than anybody else (the old golden rule: *"Them who have gold make all the rules"*). Any good office-supply store will be able to reference any of the Avery numbers listed in the window and sell you a set of labels that will work with your printer.

10. You're ready to preview the labels, so select Print Preview to look at all those little masterpieces.

HMM... The labels won't look centered on the page when you expand the print preview by clicking with the mouse (as shown in Figure 23.5), but the labels will be properly aligned when you print them to the matching Avery label.

Figure 23.5.

The full print preview.

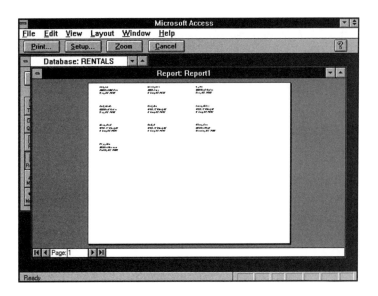

11. Save the label report under the name Tenant Labels, and take a break for the day.

YIKES!

If you need to change a report that you've created (such as rearranging the label's field placement), you can't backtrack through the ReportWizards session. You'll have to either start a new ReportWizards session or go into the report's design view and change the report's design there (which is difficult).

Chapter Wrap-Up

You are now as much of a report wizard as Access! You know all you need to know to guide Access through a report's creation, and you'll be able to make your labels look any way you want.

The most important thing to remember about labels is that you must select exactly where you want your fields to appear, not just which fields should print. You will literally point and click your way through the creation of the label, rearranging and adding anything you want before, after, or between your label's fields.

Diving In

- Use ReportWizards to create labels.

- Design the label by telling ReportWizards which fields to print and where to print them.

- Use a query for the label rather than a table if you want to print labels with data from two or more separate tables.

Sunk

- Don't think that mailing labels are the only kind of labels Access generates. Any kind of label that you need can be printed.

Part VIII
Advanced Access

Can Access
Draw Graphs?

Access Creates Beautiful Graphs
from Your Database

● *Let's Draw*   273
● *Getting a Little Bolder*   275
● *Get to Work and Play!*   277

If a picture is worth a thousand words, Access sure has a big vocabulary! Instead of having to purchase an additional program to produce colorful graphs, you can have Access produce them for you directly from the data inside your database.

Creating a graph is almost as easy as creating a form. As a matter of fact, a graph *is* a form to Access. After you create a graph, you can store it and view it as a subform inside another form.

This chapter only skims the surface of graphing with Access, but it is one of the most fun chapters in the book. Access supports many types of colorful graphs, and after you see how to design one or two, you'll want to experiment with others.

HMM... In today's boardrooms, company presidents and CEOs prefer looking at graphs, not lists of numbers. They do not have time to sift through a bunch of figures. Glance at Figure 24.1 and answer the following questions: Are sales up? Have they been going up awhile? Have the sales been rising fairly steadily? Was there ever a bad month? If you were handed a list of numbers, could you have answered those questions so quickly?

Figure 24.1.

A picture answers lots of questions!

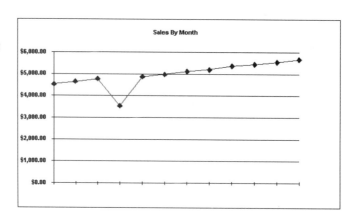

Skip This, It's Technical

Creating a meaningful graph takes some practice. Although Access supplies lots of different types of graphs, not all graphs are good for all things. *Line graphs* (such as the one in Figure 24.1) are good for showing trends. Some other graphs that Access supports are *high-low graphs*, which are excellent for stock price tracking; *bar charts* and *area charts*, which are good for looking at relationships between different fields (such as monthly sales for each division in the company); and *pie charts*, which are best used to compare single fields' values against each other (such as finding out which tenant pays the most in rent).

Let's Draw

Much of this chapter will be a review of FormWizards, so a lot of the steps will be combined into one step. Follow these instructions to graph the tenant rents as a bar chart:

1. Open the database window for the RENTALS database if it is not already open.

2. Click the Form button, and select New.

3. Select the Tenant Data table, and select FormWizards.

4. Select Graph as the form type. Cover your eyes.... Access displays its colorful window of charts like the one shown in Figure 24.2.

Figure 24.2.

Select the type of graph you want to see.

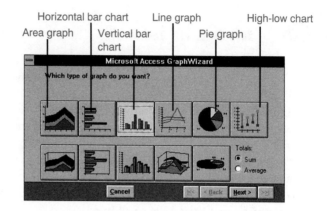

Area graph · Horizontal bar chart · Vertical bar chart · Line graph · Pie graph · High-low chart

PSST! The callouts of Figure 24.2 tell you the names of the various kinds of Access graphs. The top row contains the flat graphs (two-dimensional like a piece of paper), and the bottom row contains the fancier (but sometimes harder to figure out) 3-D graph types.

5. For the tenant data, pick the first bar graph (the third graph on the first row) by clicking its picture and choosing Next>.

6. Move the Tenant ID and the Rent Amount to the right window labeled Fields for graph, and press Next>.

7. Type `Rent Bar Chart` for the graph's title, and select Open to look at your picture! Double-click the title bar to expand the graph to full-screen, as shown in Figure 24.3.

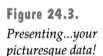

Figure 24.3.

Presenting...your picturesque data!

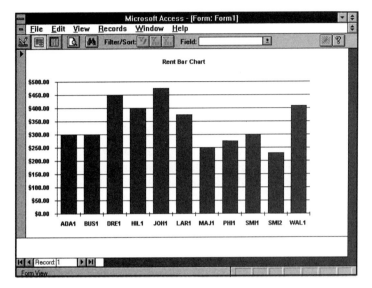

The bar chart is wonderful for zeroing in on those tenants who pay the least or the most. Access listed the bars in Tenant ID order.

8. If you want to, save the graph. However, because you'll want to create a lot of graphs and they are easy to re-create, you might want to ignore Access's request to save this particular graph.

Getting a Little Bolder

Looking at other kinds of graphs is just as easy. We are limited here because the Tenant Data table contains so little data that is of much interest for graphing. Graphs become interesting when you pit one numeric field against another as you might do when you have several tables of numeric data. However, you can create one chart with a single field; when you've got only one field to graph, nothing says *smile* like a pie chart.

1. Select a New form again, and use the Tenant Data table for the source table.

2. Select the Graph form type to display the gallery of graphs.

3. Select the pie chart (the fifth graph from the left on the top row). Again, a pie chart is useful for comparing only a single numeric field.

4. Move the Tenant ID and Deposit Amount to the right window (labeled Fields for graph), and choose Next>. Access will use the numeric field, Deposit Amount, for the pie chart, and the Tenant ID field for the labels.

5. Type My Deposit Comparison for the graph title, then click Open. After a brief pause, Access displays the pie chart shown in Figure 24.4.

Figure 24.4.

Comparing the deposits.

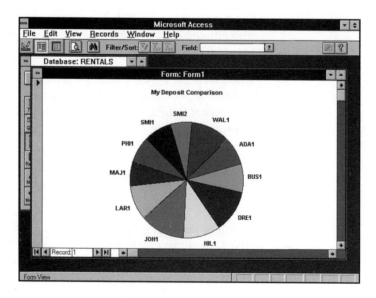

 You can see at a glance that the tenants with the IDs WAL1, DRE1, and JOH1 paid the biggest deposits, whereas tenant SMI2 didn't pay nearly as much.

Get to Work and Play!

As you add data to your own tables, you'll find more and more uses for graphs. The graphs are especially useful when you have more than one table with certain fields that need comparison. For example, if you had a northern-region customer table and a southern-region customer table, you might want to look at a 3-D bar graph of the two regions' sales to see which were the strongest.

PSST!  Of course, to pull data from two tables, first you would need to create a query that grouped the fields from the two tables into one.

Access graphs are nothing more than simple forms, and you've now worked with AccessWizards enough to understand how to create forms. You can't harm any data by creating different graphs, so feel free to experiment. After almost 25 chapters, you're ready for a graphic getaway.

PSST! Feel free to print your graph. Your Windows printer must be able to print graphics. Most printers, except for a few printers such as daisywheels, can print the Access graphs you generate. Select File Print... to print any graph being previewed on-screen.

Chapter Wrap-Up

More and more companies are relying on graphics to add impact to presentations. Although PC graphics began several years ago for games, the business and scientific world are now the true winners of the graphics tools available to us.

FormWizards includes a Graph form type that you must select before creating a graph. From the gallery of graphs Access displays on-screen, you'll select the graph that looks the best given your application's needs. After you select the fields to graph, Access takes over and draws the graph, perfectly centered in the window and ready to print or display.

Diving In

- Use FormWizards to create graphs.

- Select the type of graph that suits your needs the best.

- Create a query first if you want to graph data from two separate tables.

Sunk

- Don't select a pie chart and then choose lots of numeric fields to display on the pie chart. Pie charts are great for comparing a single field's values to each other. The remaining graph types are better for comparing more than one field at a time.

- Don't be afraid to experiment with graphs. Trying all the different types of Access graphs is the only way to learn the graphing techniques available to you.

What Lies Ahead?

Advanced Database Development, Macros, and Programming

- *Taking a Ride with Northwind Traders*   281
- *True Automation*   282
- *Macros: Your Next Step*   285

What's next? Have you come to the end of it all? *I say thee nay!* You've only just begun for this reason: Access is a multileveled database program. On the surface, the surface explored thoroughly and beyond in this book, Access is a simple database-management system with which you can create several views of your data and also generate data-entry and data-viewing forms and reports.

At the next level, the level you have now graduated to, Access becomes more than a data mover. After you develop all your tables and initial forms and reports, you've got the tedium out of the way—you've eliminated a lot of manual data tracking and record keeping. You'll be ready to automate Access using powerful auto-mating tools called *macros*.

At its most advanced level, Access is a database system that can be programmed for extremely advanced database-management capabilities. Access includes a programming language called *Access Basic* with which you can write powerful programs that handle the few involved chores that Access cannot do alone.

YIKES!

It sounds as if you've got a long way to go, doesn't it? Not necessarily. There will be people who use Access for extremely powerful and advanced database applications who will never write a single line of an Access Basic program. Program-ming is not for everybody. Not everyone is good at programming, and not everyone has the patience to learn how to program. The good news is that programming Access is the *exception* rather than the norm. Don't be in any hurry to learn Access Basic, because you might find that Access without Access Basic is all you need in order to create the database you desire.

Taking a Ride with Northwind Traders

Perhaps the thing to do now is explore a very complex database that came with your copy of Access. Microsoft included the Northwind Traders database, a database of a mythical company that shows you some of the things you can do with Access. The Northwind Traders company is a worldwide organization with customers, employees, and inventory items that all interrelate to form a huge relational database system.

Take a few moments to explore the database. Close the RENTALS database (with File Close), and open the NWIND.MDB file. Click the various buttons to the left of the database window. Right away, you'll notice something new: the database window contains so many queries, forms, and reports that they will not all fit inside the database window at the same time (even if you resize the window to full-screen)!

Try these steps on for size:

1. Click the Form button.

2. Double-click the Employees form (or highlight Employees and select Open), and stand back.... Access displays the first employee on-screen, picture and all! Enlarge the form to fill the screen (even then, you can't see the form's second half, because it is a double-page form), as shown in Figure 25.1.

3. Press Page Down to look at the form's second half. Use the record bar at the bottom of the screen to look at more employees.

Figure 25.1.

A form with a picture and everything!

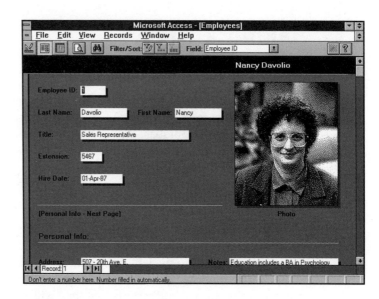

Skip This, It's Technical

Access can generate pictures from .PCX files as shown here. The picture is actually an embedded OLE Paintbrush object. Double-click the picture to go into Paintbrush. Add some highlights to the picture (like a goatee), and return to Access to view the updated record.

True Automation

If you really wanted to develop a database application for people who knew nothing about Access, you could. You can create automated forms that display when Access starts. The Northwind Traders database was not designed to start automatically when Access is loaded because the database was meant for you to see, change, and learn from—not to really use.

To see the first screen of the database if it were completely hooked up for non-database people, take these steps:

1. Close the Employees form that you are currently viewing.

2. Select the Main Switchboard and double-click the name or select the Open button.

   Access displays the Main Switchboard form, shown in Figure 25.2, from which most other activities of the database are possible. After you've looked at the main switchboard (which acts like a big graphical menu of choices for the user), click the View Forms button. You'll see another, smaller switchboard from which you can look at the database's forms.

Figure 25.2.

The starting point for the Northwind Traders database.

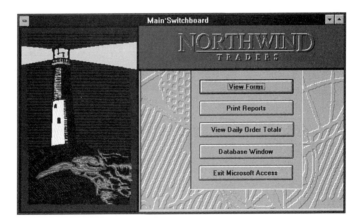

3. Click the form's Customers button, and you'll be taken to a customer form. Closing the form takes you right back to the form switchboard. By maintaining control, the form switchboard keeps the user's attention and doesn't enable the user to slip into a design view.

> **HMM...** The toolbar is still active, and because it is, the user can also move the mouse to the toolbar and click the design tool. Remember, though, that this sample database is for experimentation, not actual use. Therefore, Microsoft chose to keep the toolbar displayed in case you wanted to delve into the underlying database. There is a way to remove the toolbar to keep the user from messing things up (called *making the application bullet-proof*).

4. For one more impressive look at the Northwind Traders database, click the Categories button and scroll through the pictures of food that the database contains (Figure 25.3 shows one category being displayed).

Figure 25.3.

A category in the Northwind Traders database.

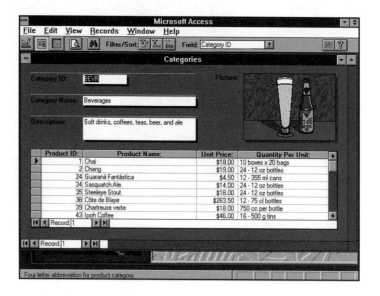

5. After you are done looking through the food, close the Categories form, and then press the colorful lighthouse on the right of the Forms Switchboard form. Access returns to the database window.

PSST! A *macro* caused the form to close when you clicked the lighthouse. The next section tells you a little about macros.

Macros: Your Next Step

After you hone the skills you learned in this book, plan to make your next education venture Access *macros*. A macro is not a programming language, and a macro is not like the keystroke-recording macros of popular spreadsheet programs on the market. A macro contains a list of predefined instructions called *actions*. Access supplies more than 40 actions you can choose from when writing a macro.

Although you'll eventually learn how to use macros to help with powerful applications such as the Northwind Traders, macros are really more useful when you find yourself repeating the same commands over and over. By creating a macro to execute those repetitive commands, you would have to only press two keys rather than repeat the same series of steps every time you wanted to do the job.

After you learn about macros, and after you've used them for a while, you might be ready to tackle Access Basic. Again, don't feel as though you need to learn Access Basic soon, because you don't. You might never need to learn it.

YIKES!

Access never really gets tough, although programming in Access Basic takes some practice. You're not going to be able to create databases like the Northwind Trader's database right away, but Access is extremely flexible. As you learn to add new features to your database, you can modify the work you've already done while affecting your data as little as possible or not at all.

Access is a database whose general features can be learned in a few hours and whose advanced commands can be challenging even for Access pros. Stick with it, create lots of databases, and you'll be ranked among members of the Access Users' Hall of Fame before you know it!

Chapter Wrap-Up

This chapter's sole goal was to whet your appetite and show you what can really be done in Access. There is no hurry. You already know enough about Access to create virtually any database. The features that you have yet to learn are the very advanced ones that you won't necessarily need to use.

Experiment as much as you can with the Northwind Traders database. If you mess it up, who cares? That's why Microsoft provided the sample database!

Diving In

- Relax, because you know enough to perform most of the tasks in any Access database no matter how small or large.

- Load, use, and modify the sample database that came with Access—the Northwind Traders database.

- Use Access as much as possible—*that's* the way you learn Access.

Sunk

- Don't jump right into Access Basic. You might never need it. Some people who are experts in other dialects of BASIC, even people who have written several books on the BASIC language (I won't mention any names...), have problems moving to Access Basic. Access Basic is difficult, and it is tough to integrate a programming language into a visual environment such as Access.

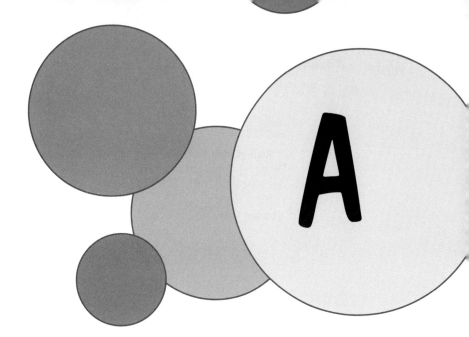

Glossary

Access Basic   The programming language supplied with Access that provides for extremely sophisticated database applications.

AccessWizards   A question/answer kind of help system built into Access. There are two kinds of AccessWizards: FormWizards and ReportWizards. The AccessWizards automate a lot of tasks.

Action query   Queries, such as the make-table query, that must be run from the toolbar or menu.

Actions   Commands inside macros that automate tasks.

Ascending order   Data sorted from the lowest value to the highest value.

Backup   A copy of your data and program files. Usually, hard disks are backed up to diskettes or tapes.

Bands   Sections of a report.

Context-sensitive help   Access includes pop-up help screens that analyze what you are doing when you request help and then give you help on the topic you are working on.

Control-menu button   The small button in the upper-left corner of every window that enables you to close, move, and resize the window.

Counter   A data type applied to primary key fields that contain unique, sequential numbers.

Cue cards   A step-by-step help system that instructs you what to do and waits for you to do it. Although cue cards are designed to be helpful for newcomers to Access, some Access beginners find that the cue cards (which cannot be moved or resized) get in the way.

Currency   The field data type that holds money amounts.

Data   Raw facts and figures.

Data types   All data fits into one of several Access data type categories, such as numeric data, dates, and text data.

Database   A collection of your data. A database program such as Access stores related data in tables, and all the tables and their reporting and data-entry tools work together to make up the database.

Datasheet   A spreadsheet-like row and column display of your data.

Date/time   The field data type that holds date and time values.

Datum   The singular for the plural word *data* (rarely used).

Default   A value that Access supplies if you don't type one of your own.

Descending order   Data sorted from the lowest value to the highest value.

Design view   The view of your table's structure, as opposed to a datasheet view or form view, that enables you to see the table's data.

DPI   An acronym for *dots per inch,* reflecting a printer's capability to produce quality output through a series of small dots.

Draft mode   The term that some printer manufacturers choose to call their printer's high-speed but lower-quality output. (There is usually a letter-quality mode to offset a printer's draft mode.)

Dynaset   The result of a query that changes every time data in the underlying tables changes.

Edit   The term applied to manually changing data.

End user   See *User.*

Field   A column of data in a table.

Field name   A name you give to every column in a table.

FormWizards   One set of the AccessWizards that creates forms for you as you help it along by answering a few questions and selecting some options.

Information   Processed and meaningful data.

Insert mode   One of two editing modes that enables you to insert characters before other characters. The characters that were already there move to the right to make room for the new ones.

Join   The process of relating two tables by a common field.

Key   See *Primary key field.*

Letter-quality mode   The term that some printer manufacturers choose to call their printer's low-speed but high-quality output. (There is usually a draft mode to offset a printer's letter-quality mode.) Letter-quality mode is also called *NLQ* (for *near letter-quality*).

Logical operators   Operators that enable you to combine more than one relational operator to create more powerful queries.

Macros   The capability of Access to automate some common tasks.

Main form   A form that includes another form (a subform) inside it.

Make-table query   A query that creates a new table rather than a dynaset.

Memo fields   Fields in a table that can contain several thousands of characters of data.

Module   An Access Basic program.

Network administrator   The person at your location who understands the ins and outs of your networked computer (if you use a networked computer) and who you can go to for help.

NLQ mode   See *Letter-quality mode.*

Objects   A general term for the primary building blocks of access: tables, queries, forms, reports, macros, and modules.

Off-site backups   The term applied to backup copies of your data that are not located in the vicinity of your computer.

OLE object   An advanced Windows feature that enables you to embed pictures, spreadsheets, and any other Windows OLE object in a database, form, or report.

Overtype mode   An editing mode that replaces characters of text as you type.

Primary key field   A field in most tables that contains unique data for each record (sometimes called the key).

Print preview   The WYSIWYG feature of Access that enables you to look at a form or report on-screen before printing to paper.

Properties   Each field has several properties, such as width, and a default value that you can specify if you like.

Query   Basically, a query is like a question of your database data. The result of the query is the answer to your question. When you want a subset of data from one or more tables, create a query, and Access produces the subset.

Query by example (QBE)   The query-building windows that lead you through the creation of a query.

Record   A row of data in a table.

Relational database management system (RDBMS)   An RDBMS is a collection of data stored in tables. All tables in a properly designed RDBMS relate by at least one field to a different field somewhere. In a well-designed RDBMS, all common data, no matter how many tables the same fields appear in, is stored in one place on the disk. If you change the data in one table, that data will be changed elsewhere as long as you have explicitly joined the tables.

Relational operators   A series of symbols that enable you to compare data so that you can extract and select only those records or fields that you need.

Report   Printed output of your data.

ReportWizards   The AccessWizards system that creates a report for you as you help it along by answering a few questions and selecting some options.

Row selector   A black arrow that points to the current record you are working with.

Secondary sort key   When sorting data, you often specify two fields to sort by. The second one, called the secondary sort key, determines how data inside a group sorts.

Select-only query   A query that results in a dynaset rather than a new table.

Sorting   Putting data, such as an alphabetized list of names, in order.

Subform   A form that appears inside another form.

Table   A collection of related records inside a database.

Text   A field data type that enables you to store a string of characters in a field. You cannot perform any calculation on a text field, even if the field contains numeric digits.

Text cursor   A vertical line that moves with the mouse over text areas and that appears as you enter characters into a field.

Toolbar   A collection of buttons at the top of your Access screen, directly beneath the menu, that offers shortcut ways to direct Access.

User   The person who uses an Access database application—not always the creator of the database (also called end user).

View   A method that Access provides that enables you to look at your table or the table definition.

WYSIWYG   Pronounced WIZZ-ee-wig, WYSIWYG is an acronym that describes the screen previewing features of Access. With WYSIWYG, you can look at a report on-screen before printing the report.

Yes/No   A field data type that can contain a yes or no (sometimes called a true or false) value that answers a question about data.

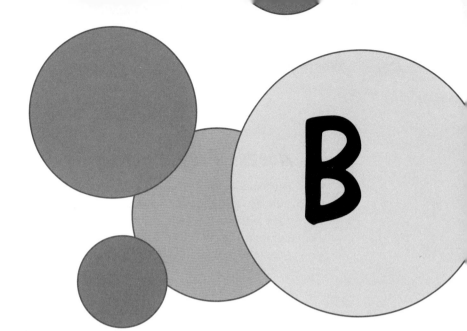

Where Do I Go from Here?

This appendix lists some books that you might want to read now that you know Access.

Teach Yourself Access in 21 Days

Users can achieve Access success now! This handy tutorial contains 21 lessons, each of which can be completed in two to three hours. Special features such as Syntax boxes, Dos and Don'ts, Q&A, and Workshop sections help reinforce the information covered in the text. Available in June 1993. (For beginning to intermediate users.)

Access Programming by Example

This book is for users who understand the fundamentals of table/database design and now want to explore Access Basic code. The book features review questions and exercises in each chapter and a glossary of common database, programming, and Access terms. Available in July 1993. (For beginning to intermediate users.)

Secrets of the Microsoft Access Masters

The ultimate guide for mastering Microsoft Access! This comprehensive guide gives readers insights into setting up database systems and developing applications that use the power of Access. The book/disk combination contains information on how to effectively use macros and develop applications with Access Basic. Available in August 1993. (For intermediate to advanced users.)

Microsoft Access Developer's Guide

Step-by-step instructions for application development with Microsoft Access. Readers can use this book/disk combination as a guide to powerful database programming. The disk contains all the programming examples listed in the text as well as other applications and utilities not found in the text.

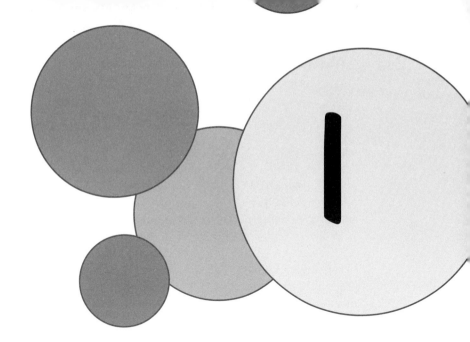

Index

Symbols

\# wildcard character, 193-195

* wildcard character, 159

< (less than) relational operator, 193-195

<= (less than or equal to) relational operator, 193-195

<> (not equal to) relational operator, 193-195

= (equal to) relational operator, 193-195

> (greater than) relational operator, 193-195

>= (greater than or equal to) relational operator, 193-195

? wildcard character, 159

A

Access, 7-9
   hardware requirements, 26-27
   installing, 26-29
      on network, 29
   publications, 293-294
   quitting, 31-32
   starting, 29-30
Access Basic, 280, 285-287
   modules, 55

accessing help, 34-38
   Contents windows, 37
   F1 function key, 36
AccessWizards, 9, 41, 287
   FormWizards, 289
      creating forms, 135-138
      customizing forms, 168
   graphs, creating, 273-277
   ReportWizards, 250-258, 291
      labels, 260-268
action queries, 234-235, 287

actions, 285-287
active fields, 96
adding, *see* inserting
aligning fields, 174
AND logical operator,
    199-200
arranging, *see*
    rearranging fields
ascending sorts, 185
asterisk (*) wildcard
    character, 159
automated forms,
    creating, 282-285
Avery label system, 266

B

backups, 86-91, 287
    off-site, 87, 290
    restoring files, 92
    SYSTEM.MDA file,
        91
bands, 170, 287
    color, changing,
        170-172
    detail, 170
    footer, 170
    header, 170
bar charts, 273-275
BETWEEN logical opera-
    tor, 200

C

closing windows, 35-36
    help windows, 35
    table definition
        window, 82

Codd, Dr. E. F., 9
colors, changing,
    170-172
columns, *see* fields
commands
    Edit menu
        Delete, 130
        Delete Row, 98
        Find, 157
        Insert Row, 97
        Replace, 159
        Undo, 98
    File menu
        Exit, 31-32
        Print, 147, 152
        Print Preview,
            129-130, 149
        Save, 81
    Help menu
        Contents, 37
        Search, 38
    Layout menu
        Gridlines, 164
        Hide Columns,
            161
        Show Columns,
            162
    Query menu
        Make Table, 233
        Run, 234
        Select, 235
    Records menu
        Data Entry, 142
        Show All Records,
            142
complex queries,
    201-204

Contents command
    (Help menu), 37
Contents window, 37
context-sensitive help,
    8, 39-40, 287
control-menu button,
    35-36, 288
controls (forms), 170
Counter fields, 65, 288
creating
    databases, 48-50
    forms, 135-138
        automated forms,
            282-285
        from queries,
            205-207
        specifying fields,
            137
        with multiple-
            query tables, 238
    graphs
        bar charts, 273-275
        pie charts, 275-277
    labels, 261-267
    multiple-table
        queries, 228-230
    queries, 182-187
    reports, 250-254
    subforms, 240-244
    tables, 60-69
        defining table,
            66-68
        field characteris-
            tics, 62-66
        from dynasets,
            233-235

criteria (query),
  matching, 190-192
    with relational
      operators, 193-195
cue cards, 34, 40, 288
currency values,
  entering in tables, 115
Currency fields, 65-66,
  288
    default value, 121
    entering data, 115
customizing forms
    colors, changing,
      170-172
    in form design view,
      169-176
    rearranging fields,
      172-175
    resizing fields,
      175-176
    with FormWizard,
      168

D

data, 4, 288
    editing, 108
      in forms, 140-141
    entering in tables,
      108-109, 218-222
        copying duplicate
          data, 127
        correcting errors,
          114
        in datasheet view,
          109-114, 120-127

    in form view,
      141-142
    special data
      considerations,
      114-115
    overlapping, 19
    replacing values,
      159-161
    searching for,
      156-159
      with wildcard
        characters, 159
Data Entry command
  (Records menu), 142
data pointers, 19, 187
data types, 288
    see also fields
database window,
  50-51, 66
    enlarging, 51
    form object, 53-54
    macro object, 55
    module object, 55
    query object, 52-53
    report object, 54
    table object, 51-52
    see also specific object
databases, 5-6, 14-15,
  288
    backing up, 86-92
      off-site backups,
        87
      restoring backups,
        92
    creating, 48-50
    Northwind Traders,
      281-285

queries, 182
    complex, 201-204
    creating, 182-187
    criteria, matching,
      190-200
    displaying
      dynasets, 187
    multiple-table,
      226-236
    running, 186-187
    selecting fields,
      184-186
    selecting tables
      for, 183
    sorts, specifying,
      185-186
records, 17-19, 291
    deleting, 130-131,
      142
    moving between,
      120, 127-128,
      139-140
    selecting for
      multiple-table
      queries, 231-233
    sorting, 128
    relational, 9, 18
    tables, see tables
datasheet view, 108
    entering data in
      tables, 109-114,
      120-127
    fields
      formatting,
        162-163
      hiding, 161-162
      rearranging, 116
      resizing, 115-116

moving between
records, 127-128
replacing data
values, 159-161
searching for data,
156-159
switching between
design view, 116
datasheets, 288
deleting records,
130-131
hiding gridlines, 164
printing, 146-148
modes, 150
page range,
specifying, 149
print preview,
129-130
specifying
records, 148
to a file, 150
Date/Time fields,
65-69, 288
dates, entering in
tables, 114
defining tables, 66-68
field properties,
78-80
naming fields, 73
specifying fields,
77-78
Delete command
(Edit menu), 130
Delete key, 77, 112, 130
Delete Row command
(Edit menu), 98

deleting
fields, 98-99
range of records, 130
records
in datasheet view,
130-131
in form view, 142
descending sorts, 185
design view, 68, 288
switching between
datasheet view, 116
detail band, 170
color, changing,
170-172
dialog boxes
Find, 157
Print, 147-150
Query Properties,
233
Replace, 159-160
Search, 38-39
directories, selecting, 49
displaying
dynasets, 187
field description, 113
DPI (dots per inch), 150,
289
draft mode, 150, 289
drives, selecting, 49
dynasets, 160, 289
creating tables from,
233-235
displaying, 187
resizing, 187

E

Edit menu commands
Delete, 130
Delete Row, 98
Find, 157
Insert Row, 97
Replace, 159
Undo, 98
editing, 289
data, 108
in forms, 140-141
labels, 267
end users, 6, 292
entering
data in tables,
108-109, 218-222
copying duplicate
data, 127
correcting errors,
114
in datasheet view,
109-114, 120-127
in form view,
141-142
special data
considerations,
114-115
see also inserting
equal to (=) relational
operator, 193-195
errors, correcting, 76-77
Exit command (File
menu), 31-32

F

F1 (Help) function key, 36
fields, 17-19, 289
    active, 96
    aligning, 174
    correcting mistakes, 76-77
    Counter, 65
    Currency, 65-66, 288
        default value, 121
        entering data, 115
    Date/Time, 65-69, 288
    deleting, 98-99
    describing, 72-76
    description, displaying, 113
    formatting, 162-163
    hiding, 161-162
    inserting, 95-98
        at end of table, 96
        between fields, 97-98
    Memo, 18, 64-69, 290
        length, 96
    names, 63, 289
    naming, 73
    Number, 65-69
    OLE Object, 65
    order, 95
    primary key, 19-21, 290
        specifying, 80-81, 218
    printing on reports, 251

properties, 290
    defining, 78-80
rearranging, 102-103
    in datasheet view, 116
    in form design view, 172-175
resizing, 100-103
    in datasheet view, 115-116
    in form design view, 175-176
selecting
    for labels, 262-263
    for queries, 184-186
sorting in labels, 265
specifying, 77-78
Text, 64-69, 292
Yes/No, 65, 292
File menu commands
    Exit, 31-32
    New Database, 48
    Print, 147, 152
    Print Preview, 129-130, 149
    Save, 81
filenames, 50
    .MDB extension, 47
files
    NWIND.MDB, 281
    printing datasheets to, 150
    SYSTEM.MDA, backing up, 91
Find command (Edit menu), 157
Find dialog box, 157

footer band, 170
form design view, 169-176
    changing colors in forms, 170-172
    enlarging, 169
    rearranging fields, 172-175
    resizing fields, 175-176
form view
    deleting records, 142
    inserting data in tables, 141-142
    moving between records, 139-140
    printing from, 150-151
    switching to datasheet view, 139
formats, table, 17-19
formatting fields, 162-163
forms, 53-54, 134
    aligning fields, 174
    automated, creating, 282-285
    bands, 170
    controls, 170
    creating, 135-138
        from queries, 205-207
        specifying fields, 137
        with multiple-query tables, 238
    criteria selection, adding, 198-204

customizing
    colors, changing,
        170-172
    in form design
        view, 169-176
    rearranging fields,
        172-175
    resizing fields,
        175-176
    with FormWizard,
        168
data
    editing, 140-141
    inserting, 141-142
deleting records, 142
designing from
    scratch, 176
linking to queries,
    205
main, 238, 290
printing, 150-151
resizing, 242
saving, 142-143
scrolling, 243
selecting design, 136
subforms, 238, 292
    creating, 240-244
    moving, 244
    relating tables,
        238-240
tabular, 205
titles, 138
FormWizards, 289
    creating forms,
        135-138
    customizing forms,
        168

graphs, creating
    bar charts, 273-275
    pie charts, 275-277
    printing graphs,
        277

G

graphs, 272-278
    bar charts, 273-275
    high-low graphs, 273
    line graphs, 273
    pie charts, 273-277
    printing, 277
    type, selecting, 274
    uses, 277
greater than (>)
    relational operator,
        193-195
greater than or equal to
    (>=) relational
    operator, 193-195
gridlines, hiding, 164
Gridlines command
    (Layout menu), 164
grouping reports,
    252-257
    by numeric fields,
        256

H

hardware requirements,
    26-27
header band, 170
    color, changing,
        170-172

help, 8, 34
    accessing, 34-38
        Contents window,
            37
        F1 function key,
            36
    AccessWizards, 41
    closing help
        windows, 35
    context-sensitive, 8,
        39-40, 287
    cue cards, 34, 40, 288
    searching for topics,
        38-39
Help menu commands
    Contents, 37
    Search, 38
Help window, 35
Hide Columns
    command (Layout
    menu), 161
hiding
    fields, 161-162
    gridlines, 164
high-low graphs, 273

I

information, 4, 289
Insert key, 112
Insert mode, 77, 289
Insert Row command
    (Edit menu), 97
inserting
    fields, 95-98
        at end of table, 96
        between fields,
            97-98

tables, 217-218
see also entering
installing Access, 26-29
on network, 29

J–K

joining tables, 227-228, 289
specifying common field, 227
with mouse, 229

L

labels, 260-268
adding extra text, 265
Avery label system, 266
editing, 267
generating, 261-267
moving between lines, 263
previewing, 266
punctuation, 264
selecting fields, 262-263
sorting fields, 265
see also reports
Layout menu commands
Gridlines, 164
Hide Columns, 161
Show Columns, 162
less than (<) relational operator, 193-195

less than or equal to (<=) relational operator, 193-195
letter-quality mode, 150, 289
line graphs, 273
linking forms to queries, 205
logical operators, 198-200, 289
AND, 199-200
BETWEEN, 200
OR, 200
Long Date format, 162-163

M

macros, 55, 280, 285-290
actions, 285-287
mailing labels, 260-268
adding extra text, 265
Avery label system, 266
editing, 267
generating, 261-267
moving between lines, 263
previewing, 266
punctuation, 264
selecting fields, 262-263
sorting fields, 265
main form, 238, 290
scrolling, 243

Make Table command (Query menu), 233
make-table queries, 290
creating, 233-235
many-to-many table relationships, 216
.MDB filename extension, 47
Memo fields, 18, 64-69, 290
length, 96
modes
draft, 150, 289
Insert, 77, 289
letter-quality, 150, 289
Overtype, 77, 290
modules, 55, 290
mouse, 27
joining tables, 229
rearranging fields, 102-103
resizing fields, 100-103
moving
between label lines, 263
between records
in datasheet view, 120, 127-128
in form view, 139-140
fields (form design view), 172-175
subforms, 244
text cursor, 73

multiple tables
  queries, 226-236
    creating, 228-230
    forms, creating,
      238
    joining tables,
      227-228
    make-table
      queries, 233-235
    running, 234
    selecting records,
      231-233
  relating, 212-216
    many-to-many
      relationships,
      216
    one-to-many
      relationships,
      214-215
    one-to-one
      relationships,
      213

N

names
  fields, 63, 289
  tables, 68
naming fields, 73
networks
  network administra-
    tor, 290
  installing Access, 29
New Database com-
  mand (File menu), 48
New Database window,
  48-49

Northwind Traders
  database, 281-285
not equal to (<>)
  relational operator,
  193-195
Number fields, 65-69
NWIND.MDB file, 281

O

objects, 47-51, 290
  forms, 53-54
  macros, 55
  modules, 55
  queries, 52-53
  reports, 54
  tables, 51-52
  see also specific object
off-site backups, 87, 290
OLE (Object Linking
  and Embedding), 290
OLE Object fields, 65
one-to-many
  table relationships,
  214-215, 238-240
one-to-one table
  relationships, 213
operators
  logical, 198-200, 289
  relational, 193-195,
  291
OR logical operator, 200
order of fields, 95
overlapping data, 19
Overtype mode, 77, 290

P

pie charts, 273-277
pound sign (#) wildcard
  character, 193-195
primary key fields,
  19-21, 290
  specifying, 80-81, 218
Print command (File
  menu), 147, 152
Print dialog box,
  147-150
print preview, 129-130
  datasheets, 129
  labels, 266
  reports, 252-253
Print Preview
  command (File
  menu), 129-130, 149
printer modes, 289
printing
  datasheets, 146-148
    modes, 150
    page range,
      specifying, 149
    print preview,
      129-130
    specifying
      records, 148
    to a file, 150
  fields, on reports, 251
  forms, 150-151
  graphs, 277
  mailing labels,
    260-268
  reports, 253

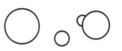

properties (field), 290
  defining, 78-80
publications (Access),
  293-294

Q

QBE (Query By
  Example), 53, 201-204,
  291
queries, 52-53, 182, 291
  action, 234-235, 287
  complex, 201-204
  creating, 182-187
  creating forms from,
    205-207
  criteria, matching,
    190-192
    with logical
      operators,
      198-200
    with relational
      operators,
      193-195
  dynasets
    creating tables
      from, 233-235
    displaying, 187
    resizing, 187
  make-table, 290
    creating, 233-235
  multiple-table,
    226-236
    creating, 228-230
    forms, creating,
      238

  joining tables,
    227-228
    running, 234
    selecting records,
      231-233
  running, 186-187
  select-only, 235, 291
  selecting fields, 184
  selecting tables for,
    183
  sorts, specifying,
    185-186
Query By Example
  (QBE), 53, 201-204, 291
Query menu
  commands
    Make Table, 233
    Run, 234
    Select, 235
Query Properties dialog
  box, 233
quitting Access, 31-32

R

ranges of records,
  deleting, 130
RDBMS (relational
  database management
  system), 8, 291
rearranging fields,
  102-103
  in datasheet view,
    116
  in form design view,
    172-175

records, 17-19, 291
  deleting
    in datasheet view,
      130-131
    in form view, 142
  moving between
    in datasheet view,
      120, 127-128
    in form view,
      139-140
  range of, deleting,
    130
  selecting for
    multiple-table
    queries, 231-233
  sorting, 128
Records menu
  commands
    Data Entry, 142
    Show All Records,
      142
relating tables, 212-216,
  238-240
  many-to-many
    relationships, 216
  multiple-table
    queries, 226-236
    creating, 228-230
    creating tables
      from dynasets,
      233-235
    joining tables,
      227-228
    selecting records,
      231-233

one-to-many
relationships,
214-215, 238-240
one-to-one
relationships, 213
relational database
management system
(RDBMS), 8, 291
relational databases, 9,
18
relational operators,
193-195, 291
Replace command
(Edit menu), 159
Replace dialog box,
159-160
replacing data values,
159-161
reports, 54, 291
bands, 287
creating, 250-254
grouping, 252-257
by numeric fields,
256
previewing, 252-253
printing, 253
printing fields, 251
sorting, 252
titles, 252
type, selecting, 251
see also labels
ReportWizards,
250-258, 291
labels, 260-268
adding extra text,
265
editing, 267

generating labels,
261-267
previewing, 266
punctuation, 264
selecting fields,
262-263
sorting fields, 265
see also reports
resizing
dynasets, 187
fields, 100-103
in datasheet view,
115-116
in form design
view, 175-176
forms, 242
restoring backed-up
files, 92
row selector, 96, 291
rows, see records
ruler guides, aligning
fields, 174
Run command
(Query menu), 234
running queries,
186-187
multiple-table
queries, 234

S

Save command
(File menu), 81
saving
forms, 142-143
tables, 81-82

screens, see windows
Search command (Help
menu), 38
Search dialog box, 38-39
searching
for data, 156-159
with wildcard
characters, 159
help topics, 38-39
secondary sort key, 291
Select command
(Query menu), 235
Select Query window,
183
select-only queries, 235,
291
selecting
directories, 49
drives, 49
fields
for labels, 262, 263
for queries,
184-186
form design, 136
graph type, 274
records for multiple-
table queries,
231-233
tables for queries,
183
Show All Records
command (Records
menu), 142
Show Columns
command (Layout
menu), 162

sizing
  dynasets, 187
  fields, 100-103
    in datasheet view,
      115-116
    in form design
      view, 175-176
  forms, 242
sorting, 185, 291
  ascending sorts, 185
  descending sorts, 185
  fields in labels, 265
  records, 128
  reports, 252
starting Access, 29-30
startup window, 30
subforms, 238, 292
  creating, 240-244
  moving, 244
  relating tables,
    238-240
  scrolling, 243
SYSTEM.MDA file,
  backing up, 91

T

table definition
  window, 67
  closing, 82
  describing fields,
    72-76
  enlarging, 67
tables, 16-17, 51-52, 292
  creating, 60-69
    defining table,
      66-68

field characteris-
  tics, 62-66
  from dynasets,
    233-235
data, entering,
  108-115, 218-222
  in datasheet view,
    120-127
defining, 66-68
enlarging, 67
fields, 17-19, 289
  active, 96
  aligning, 174
  correcting
    mistakes, 76-77
  Counter, 65
  Currency, 65-66
  Date/Time, 65-69
  defining proper-
    ties, 78-80
  deleting, 98-99
  describing, 72-76
  formatting,
    162-163
  hiding, 161-162
  inserting, 95-98
  Memo, 18, 64-69,
    290
  naming, 73
  Number, 65-69
  OLE Object, 65
  order, 95
  primary keys,
    19-21, 80-81, 290
  rearranging,
    102-103

resizing, 100-103
selecting for
  queries, 184-186
specifying, 77-78
Text, 64-69, 292
Yes/No, 65, 292
format, 17-19
inserting, 217-218
joining, 227-228
  specifying com-
    mon field, 227
  with mouse, 229
multiple-table
  queries, 226-236
  creating, 228-230
  forms, creating,
    238
  joining tables,
    227-228
  make-table
    queries, 233-235
  selecting records,
    231-233
names, 68
overlapping data, 19
print preview,
  129-130
records, 17-19, 291
  deleting, 130-131
  moving between,
    120, 127-128
  selecting for
    multiple-table
    queries, 231-233
  sorting, 128

relating, 212-216, 238-240
  many-to-many relationships, 216
  one-to-many relationships, 214-215, 238-240
  one-to-one relationships, 213
saving, 81-82
selecting for queries, 183
zooming, 130
tabular forms, 205
text cursor, 292
  insert mode, 77
  moving, 73
  overtype mode, 77
Text fields, 64-69, 292
time, entering in tables, 114
titles
  form titles, 138
  report titles, 252
toolbar, 35, 292
tools, *see* objects

U

Undo command (Edit menu), 98
undoing mistakes, 76-77, 98
users, 6, 292

V

views, 292
datasheet, 108
  entering data in tables, 109-114, 120-127
  formatting fields, 162-163
  hiding fields, 161-162
  moving between records, 127-128
  rearranging fields, 116
  replacing data values, 159-161
  resizing fields, 115-116
  searching for data, 156-159
  switching between design view, 116
design, 68, 288
  switching between datasheet view, 116
form
  deleting records, 142
  inserting data in tables, 141-142
  moving between records, 139-140
  printing from, 150-151
  switching to datasheet view, 139
form design, 169-176
  changing colors in forms, 170-172
  enlarging, 169
  rearranging fields, 172-175
  resizing fields, 175-176

W

wildcard characters
  # (pound sign), 193-195
  * (asterisk), 159
  ? (question mark), 159
Windows, backups, 88-91
windows
  closing, 36
  Contents, 37
  database, 50-55, 66
    enlarging, 51
    form object, 53-54
    macro object, 55
    module object, 55
    query object, 52-53
    report object, 54
    table object, 51-52
    see also specific object

Help, 35
New Database, 48-49
Select Query, 183
startup, 30
table definition, 67
   closing, 82
   describing fields,
    72-76
   enlarging, 67
WYSIWYG, 7, 292

X–Y–Z

Yes/No fields, 65, 292

zooming datasheet, 130

Add to Your Sams Library Today with the Best Books for Programming, Operating Systems, and New Technologies

The easiest way to order is to pick up the phone and call

1-800-428-5331

between 9:00 a.m. and 5:00 p.m. EST.

For faster service please have your credit card available.

ISBN	Quantity	Description of Item	Unit Cost	Total Cost
0-672-30318-3		Windows Sound FunPack (book/disk)	$19.95	
0-672-30310-8		Windows Graphics FunPack (book/disk)	$19.95	
0-672-30345-0		Wasting Time with Windows (book/disk)	$19.95	
0-672-30298-5		Windows NT: The Next Generation	$22.95	
0-672-30190-3		Windows Resource and Memory Management (book/disk)	$29.95	
0-672-27366-7		Memory Management for All of Us	$29.95	
0-672-30240-3		OS/2 2.1 Unleashed (book/disk)	$34.95	
0-672-30288-8		DOS Secrets Unleashed (book/disk)	$39.95	
0-672-30269-1		Absolute Beginner's Guide to Programming	$19.95	
0-672-30326-4		Absolute Beginner's Guide to Networking	$19.95	
0-672-30341-8		Absolute Beginner's Guide to C	$16.95	
0-672-30259-4		Do-It-Yourself Visual Basic for Windows, 2E	$24.95	
0-672-30229-2		Turbo C++ for Windows Programming for Beginners (book/disk)	$39.95	
0-672-30040-0		Teach Yourself C in 21 Days	$24.95	
0-672-30324-8		Teach Yourself QBasic in 21 Days	$24.95	
0-672-30249-7		Multimedia Madness! (book/disk/CD-ROM)	$44.95	
0-672-30248-9		FractalVision (book/disk)	$39.95	
❏ 3½" Disk		Shipping and Handling: See information below.		
❏ 5¼" Disk		TOTAL		

Shipping and Handling: $4.00 for the first book, and $1.75 for each additional book. Floppy disk: add $1.75 for shipping and handling. If you need to have it *now*, we can ship product to you in 24 hours for an additional charge of approximately $18.00, and you will receive your item overnight or in two days. Overseas shipping and handling adds $2.00 per book and $8.00 for up to three disks. Prices subject to change. Call for availability and pricing information on latest editions.

11711 N. College Avenue, Suite 140, Carmel, Indiana 46032

1-800-428-5331 — Orders   1-800-835-3202 — FAX   1-800-858-7674 — Customer Service

Book ISBN 0-672-30366-3